KAT

THE
JOYS
OF JET LAG

HOW TO USE A TRAVELER'S MINDSET
TO NOT BE AN A✈HOLE IN DAILY LIFE

Published by Joysetter Media.

For more information, please contact:
hello@joysettermedia.com | www.katmedina.com

ISBN 979-8-9868763-0-6 (Paperback)
ISBN 979-8-9868763-2-0 (Ebook)
ISBN 979-8-9868763-1-3 (Audiobook)

First edition

Publisher's Cataloging-in-Publication Data

Names: Medina, Kat, author.

Title: The joys of jet lag : how to use a traveler's mindset to not be an a-hole in daily life / Kat Medina.

Description: South Lake Tahoe, CA: Joysetter Media, 2022.

Identifiers: LCCN: 2022916566 | ISBN: 979-8-9868763-0-6 (paperback) | 979-8-9868763-2-0 (ebook) | 979-8-9868763-1-3 (audio)

Subjects: LCSH: Happiness. | Conduct of life. | Self-actualization (Psychology). | Travel—Psychological aspects. | Self-help.

BISAC: SELF-HELP / Motivational & Inspirational. | SELF-HELP / Personal Growth / Happiness. | SELF-HELP / Spiritual. | TRAVEL / Special Interest / Adventure.

Classification: LCC BF637.S4 .M44 2022 | DDC 158.1--dc23

Cover and interior design by Sar Dugan

JOYSETTER
MEDIA

For River.
You're the greatest joy of my life.

TABLE OF CONTENTS

INTRODUCTION
PREPARE FOR TAKEOFF

The tiny beat-up Datsun taxi sped through the winding mountain roads high in the Andes. The driver, blasting salsa music, barely let off the gas as he passed other drivers, oblivious to the "Do Not Pass" signs that dotted the mountainside. A quick two honks followed by making the sign of the cross over his body was sufficient luck to pass on the countless blind turns. Too bad I wasn't Catholic; I had to rely solely on the hope of honks. On the righthand side of the road stood a steep mountain wall with the occasional remnants of a recent landslide, and on the left, a severe drop down a thousand-foot ravine, without a single guardrail to obstruct the view or save an unlucky car. The cool, crisp mountain air blended with the smell of burning trash from the tiny, corrugated metal shack homes we passed. I understood instantly how different my life was about to be.

It was January 2012, and I had arrived at a small Ecuadorian airport about 30 minutes prior with a large suitcase, my trusty orange and brown North Face backpack, and the same nervous hopefulness that had guided me on this adventure: six months in South America as a solo 26-year-old female.

I had always been passionate about traveling, and as a child I had dreamed not of walking down the aisle with prince charming, but of becoming an explorer of the world's far-off places. Travel was equal to happiness for me. This trip to South America was one of my many solo adventures abroad. I was driven by a deep desire to feel the aliveness that comes from going to a place where I didn't know a soul and perceiving life with refreshing novelty. It was during that trip to Ecuador that I first noticed the differences between who I was on my travels and who I was at home.

We all know that feeling—the easygoing joy that naturally arises on a trip. We watch the world around us with curiosity, awed by unfamiliarity. The unexpected setbacks that we inevitably encounter are viewed as part of the adventure. We can accept them with humor, knowing they will become the elements of a good story. We participate in the moment at hand and uplift it by being openhearted. We meet new people, try new things, and appreciate the differences rather than avoiding or condemning them.

And then our trip ends, and we return home. We fall back into our routine, attempting to control the uncontrollable, seeing challenges as unfair personal attacks from life, and becoming blind to the wonders and gifts around us because we've grown so accustomed to having them.

Basically, we go into asshole autopilot, settling for a life of mediocrity that's occasionally sprinkled with the brief and fleeting joy from a recent vacation. Before we know it, life will have passed us by and we're guaranteed to look back with defeated eyes of regret, wondering *what if*. What if we had actually listened to the voice within, desperately begging us to find genuine happiness in the now, to pursue that which fulfills us, instead of burying it out of fear or doubt?

Discomfort awakens our capacity for wonder. When we explore beyond the outer limits of our comfort zone, we can once again see life with fresh eyes. Our senses absorb the differences around us, requiring us to pay attention and be present. Adventure grips hold of our spirit, shaking the long-dormant part of our authentic self that was forced into hibernation by the monotony of our daily lives.

My journey to South America woke up a part of me that could never again be contained—the wild, authentic piece of me that craved the raw beauty that is only possible when we feel we're living fully.

As my trip neared its end, I decided to make it my mission to bridge the gap between who I was when I traveled and who I was at home. I examined the values and beliefs that I effortlessly embodied on my travels to more than 30 countries and applied them to my daily life. I noticed that when I adopted a traveler's mindset, there was an undeniable impact on the quality of my life. A simple shift in my thinking completely transformed the way I saw the world. I began to appreciate the journey as much as the destination. I began to live fully.

The Joys of Jet Lag is a guide to telling your inner asshole to suck it so you can create more joy in the day-to-day. It explores the values that constitute a traveler's mindset and provides you with the tools and insights for living your best life, one of wholehearted adventure and unbridled joy, no matter where you are.

Life is happening all around you, just waiting for you to open up and take a step out of your daily routine and into the unknown. It is during those brief moments of trust that the magic happens. I hope this book helps you to see it.

CHAPTER ONE
OPENHEARTED

NEPAL

I adjusted my headlamp, zipped my red jacket, and pushed open the heavy door as I stepped into a blast of cool air. The stars were twinkling, and the moon was full enough to bathe the uneven, rocky path in a pale glow. Wind rustled the faded, once-colorful Tibetan prayer flags dancing softly in the early morning breeze. My friend Amber and I were on the second-to-last day of our four-day trek through the Annapurna region of Nepal, having awakened at four in the morning to hike to the top of Poon Hill in Ghorepani (pervy name, cool place). Several travelers joined us on the trail as we sleepily put one foot in front of the other in near silence. We were hoping for clear skies and an incredible sunrise, both of which were uncommon for that time of year. Shuffling through the darkness, it left time for the flowing thoughts that seem to naturally come about in hours typically spent sleeping.

I thought about the randomness of life. How imperfectly perfect every moment was and how seemingly fortuitous moments of openheartedness can lead to the most incredible unforeseen adventures. I felt like a leaf in a river. If I resisted life's subtle guidance, it was as though I was blocked behind a rock of my own making. Whenever I let go, trusted, and said yes to whatever was in front of me with a receptive and open heart and mind, I would float onward, exactly to where I was meant to be. Life seemed to be a balance of surrender and drive. Coincidences seemed to be more like trail markers, offering the choice to continue straight ahead or veer off course and retreat. Each would lead to my destiny, but one tended to have serendipitous magic sprinkled along the way. I was learning how to trust.

So much of my life had been dedicated to achieving the goals or expectations that I had set for myself. I white-knuckled my way through countless situations, set on doing things the way I had intended and forcing it to go the way I thought was best. Occasionally, I would open up enough to let grace in. I would say yes to something that wasn't on the "life schedule." I would be open to a random conversation with a stranger, or an invitation to something out of my comfort zone. I realized that in those moments of discomfort I was shifting into a receptive mindset of growth and openness. I was allowing my inner voice of guidance to speak and be heard. The more I listened to it, the more it would speak up. The more I said yes, the more magic I would find. I was beginning to question whether all the rigid controlling I felt I had to do to achieve what I wanted was actually necessary. What if it was meant to be easier?

After about an hour of hiking, we arrived at the top of Poon Hill just as the sky was beginning to shift from night to day. It was a dimly lit blanket of grayish-purple light that was evolving and transforming with every blink. The air was filled with anticipation and excitement. The previous day was cloudy, cold, and raining with minimal visibility minus the occasional peekaboo of a rocky mountainside or a glimpse of the green valley floor thousands of feet below. Already, we could see the many peaks of the Annapurna range, clouds moving quickly as if they were trying to clear offstage in time for the big arrival of the main star. We settled into a spot that wasn't too crowded and waited for the sunrise. It was a balance of appreciating the moment and looking forward to the next. Two stray mountain dogs played amongst the hikers, who warmed their hands on the sweet and spicy blend of masala tea sold from a lone shack nearby.

Slowly, steadily, the sun rose, and the clouds moved lower to unveil the massive mountains in their full glory. The snowy mountain faces began to light up with a golden pink glow as the sun spread against their surface one by one. Hikers let out a collective gasp of awe. It felt like such an intimate moment and we, dozens of perfect strangers from all over the world, experienced it as one. Connected in a moment that would be forever ingrained in our memory, and a reminder of the beauty of life.

The clouds framed the mountains so they appeared to float in the sky, almost as though we were looking at another planet. They stood at just over 26,000 feet in elevation, and with us at a mere 10,000 feet, they had an almost otherworldly effect. To be so high up and yet looking at something 2.5 times higher filled me with indescribable appreciation. It was beautiful. It was in that moment of incredulous wonder that I felt consumed by gratitude. How lucky was I to be witnessing this? The odds of a picture-perfect sunrise with fantastic conditions were slim to none considering the forecast. And yet, with a balance of drive and trust—continuing on hiking, hoping, appreciating the journey—we were gifted with the results of surrender at its finest.

OPENING UP

For as long as I can remember, my need to control has led me to white-knuckle my way through life. It's enabled me to accomplish so many things that initially felt far-off and nearly impossible. And yet I knew that if I set up a plan, created the steps, and followed through at all costs, I could force it to happen. I left no room for life to intersect. But the magic that waits patiently to present itself needs an opportunity to appear. A subtle change. An event that may come out of the blue and perhaps mask itself as a problem or some deterrent from the goal at hand, such that it is all too often overlooked, avoided, and resisted.

So many moments had showed up in my life as a hidden opportunity for assistance and guidance, but I had ignored them, thinking that they would take me away from my goals.

What if our entire life was spent in a way that doesn't serve us? What if we misunderstood what life was really all about? What if the point is to learn to let go, to free up moments that allow life to step in? What if the key to living a full life is to be openhearted and receptive to all that comes our way instead of always trying to fight it?

When being openhearted is adopted as a core value and daily habit, it has the potential to drastically transform our lives by surrendering to the present moment. To be openhearted is to be receptive and open to all that comes our way. It's the act of trusting in life and letting go of the need to control. It's the result of connecting with what is true in each of us—the natural, yet often forgotten, state of being that embodies gratitude, joy, love, kindness, connection, and generosity. When we're openhearted, we get out of the analytical mind and into the strength and vulnerability of the heart. It enables us to see with clarity. It primes us to be open to new experiences and interactions that come into our lives serendipitously. Openheartedness allows us to take a break from being a judgy dick, and instead lean into whatever the reality is at that moment. We can go with the flow of life, which allows us to be guided to exactly where we're meant to go.

When we're babies, we are naturally openhearted. We look at the world with curiosity and continue to learn and grow while accepting what is. Then, as we grow older, we are molded into a person who can function in society and contribute in some way. During that process, we learn to avoid pain and strive for pleasure, using that metric as our guiding compass in action and thought. The inevitable painful experiences in life, though intended for us to learn and better ourselves, often lead us to close off our hearts as a means of protection. Many times, we completely miss the lesson.

The problem is that the protection we have attempted to provide ourselves is actually what damages us most. A cold, callous wall begins to form around our heart to protect us from the next painful experience. A closed heart prevents us from developing meaningful connections and experiencing life fully. We must learn to welcome moments of struggle and pain wholeheartedly and recognize that even though they might hurt, they have the potential to lead us to the life we were meant to live. A life beyond the limits of mediocrity.

By adopting an openhearted approach to life, you'll open

yourself up to the life of greatness you deserve. That life will still have painful moments, but they will sure as fuck be worth it. That is what living a wholehearted life of adventure is all about. Not muting the experiences so you can remain comfortable, but committing to a life in which you embrace the vulnerability of an exposed heart. Doing so is an act of courage and strength. When we face the fear of pain or hurt and actively choose to stay open, we strengthen our resilience. We begin to examine each moment as an opportunity, a gift. We start to search for the lesson to be learned and opportunities to practice our values of love, compassion, gratitude, and humor. We begin to notice the magic in the ordinary.

Opening your heart unlocks the doors to a fulfilling, outstanding life. Sounds pretty rad, right? But how the hell do you do this?

To start, think of moments in which you were closed off and notice that there was always the option to choose the opposite: being openhearted. Maybe one of your friends invites you to a get-together with a bunch of folks you don't know. You have big plans to put on some sweatpants and Netflix and Chill in the literal sense of the phrase: solo and binge-ready. Maybe you're introverted, and the thought of meeting new people makes your butt pucker in anxiety. It's in the moment that you notice fear creeping into your decision-making that you must act.

If something seems uncomfortable or scary, it's an opportunity to kindly push yourself to learn and grow. It's life telling you to sack up. Use the possibility of discomfort to guide you to where you need to go. If it scares you, maybe you should try it out. The moment you face fear head on and move past it is the moment that fear loses its power. Courage gets stronger with practice, and creating momentum allows you to grow in ways you never could have imagined.

So, let's say you step up and decide to go to your friend's get-together. Two outcomes would be possible. Option #1: You approach it with an open heart and end up meeting some folks that you wouldn't have otherwise. You persist in maintaining openheartedness through discomfort and end up making several meaningful connections. You feel proud of yourself and take the first step towards creating momentum in overcoming fear. It leads you to move forward into another situation that asks for openheartedness, and puts you onto a beautifully unpredictable path through life.

Option #2: You go, and it's a total disaster. You're super awkward and uncomfortable, and spend more time by the snack table than with other humans (this is my go-to move when I let shyness consume me—food is always friendly, just sayin'). You feel embarrassed and stupid. Does that mean it was a mistake to go? Not even close. You tried, and even though you shit the bed, trying is the most important thing. Each time you step into those moments of discomfort, you get better and stronger. It gets easier. Be compassionate with yourself and proud that you made one big step forward toward openhearted decision-making just by getting out of your house. The true failure is not trying, which keeps you stagnant in a life that was meant for growth. And that is no way to live.

In my attempts to learn how to let go of control and live with an open heart, I began to read whatever I could on the topic of surrender. I first learned about it in greater depth thanks to Michael Singer's book *The Surrender Experiment*. It describes how to let go of one's preferences to life's events and instead surrender to whatever is placed before you. Regardless of how difficult, unfair, or upsetting the situation may be, let go of your reaction to it and just go with the flow of life. Singer mentions that the more you try to resist something, the more change it will inflict on your life or yourself, which is why you might be resisting it. He emphasizes that life has a much greater plan for us than we could ever imagine, so we might as well surrender and see where it takes us.

When I read this, I looked back at the many moments in my life that led me somewhere I never could have imagined or planned. So many of the situations that seemed to be created by chance actually appeared to hold monumental depth in the course of my life. The week before starting my freshman year of college, I broke my right ankle wakeboarding. I had to get surgery and was stuck with a non-weight-bearing cast for about a month. I ended up getting assigned to the third floor of my dorm, which meant hopping up and down three flights of stairs the first month of school (my left leg got cartoonishly buff). It seemed like a big pain in the ass at the time. But looking back with fresh eyes, I was able to see that it led me to meet my now-husband, who also happened to love wakeboarding, since it was my cast that initiated our first conversation.

When we take a moment to reflect on life's unplanned events, especially the ones that have rattled us to our core, we can see the zigzagging hidden path that has guided us to so many things that we never could have planned. It makes me wonder how many missed moments occurred because my preferences prevented me from being guided to something greater. I am very goal-oriented and pride myself on my ability to reach the milestones I set for myself. I plow through obstacles, pushing forward toward achievement. Eventually, I reach my goal and appreciate the grit and determination that helped me accomplish it. But I began to wonder if all that forceful forward motion was necessary. What would have happened if I surrendered to the roadblocks? Would it still have led me to reach my goal, or perhaps pushed me to something greater? How do we know when to surrender and when to push? Is forcing an outcome the wrong way to live?

The answer comes down to what is within our heart. If we're able to sit with ourselves and let a stillness come over us, we're able to provide a platform for our heart to speak I get that this sounds a little "airy-fairy," so another way to describe it is to swap heart for gut. What does your gut reaction say? We all have intuition, which has been an aspect of the human experience from the very beginning, meant to help humans survive. Hair standing up on the back of our necks and a tightening of our stomachs alerted us when danger was near. It was also meant to help humans thrive. The more you acknowledge your inner voice, the more clearly it will be able to communicate with you. The trick is to politely tell the rational mind to shut up so that you can hear your inner wisdom more clearly.

Typically, in the crucial fight/flight/freeze situations in life when we feel close to danger (e.g. the moments before the impact of a car accident) time seems to slow down immensely.

All of our senses are activated and our body responds without our mind guiding it. This is the part of ourselves we must channel to get the guidance we need to thrive. It is the place of quiet where time is slightly slowed and distorted, and we can connect with our inner voice.

One of the ways to access this space is by observing your thoughts and letting them go without getting sucked into their constant distraction. A simple exercise to help you practice this involves viewing your thoughts as an observer. As the thoughts arise, picture them moving by your mind and floating away without grasping onto them. Watch each thought with detached curiosity. Keep letting them drift on by without concerning yourself with the outcome. Try this for just a couple of minutes. With practice, you will find the steady stream may turn into a trickle. Each time you can bring yourself back to the empty space between the thoughts, as opposed to the thought itself, is a "rep." That is your mental bicep curl. This effort will carry over into your daily life and your decision-making. It will enable you to more easily differentiate between surrendering to pivot and surrendering to push forward, simply by providing you with a pause before reacting.

Painful moments are inevitable. Moments of fear, despair, anger, injustice, and doubt are elements of the human experience. So, knowing they will happen no matter what we do and what our goals may be, perhaps it would be wise to learn how to experience them with grace and accept them as reality. It is the way it is, and no matter how pissed off or bummed out it makes us, it cannot be changed. Our first reaction may be to wish the outcome was different. So, let's observe that reaction with curiosity. Let that feeling be felt. Accept it and look at it with compassion and interest. Just observe and ask yourself:

- What does this emotion feel like physically?
- What is going through my mind as I feel it?
- How does my body react?
- What is my breathing like?
- Am I tensing up?
- Are my thoughts racing?
- Do I feel the need to defend myself?

The more we try to stifle a feeling, the more it builds up behind the scenes. This only makes it stronger, and more demanding that it be felt and heard the next time it crops up. If we allow ourselves to notice whatever comes up with inquisitiveness, then we are able to let it go more easily. Once we let the initial reaction to the situation pass through us, we can examine the event with more clarity. It's almost as though we can separate ourselves once we let the personal preference pass. When we accept and detach, we can begin to see the path that is presented before us and get a glimpse of where we are meant to go.

Many times, we'll see that the emotional reactions we have to life's events are rooted in one thing: fear. If you really examine anger, you will begin to see that it is a public representation of feeling scared shitless. Scared of not being seen, loved, accepted, or enough. Fear, and each of its many projections, needs to be handled with compassion, which is one of fear's antidotes. Compassion is an acknowledgement that we are all in this together. We all want to be loved, to be enough, and to be seen and heard. When we are compassionate toward ourselves and others, especially when responding to a projection of fear, we can begin to heal the wounds of separateness. Compassion allows us to focus on our human commonalities and connect over those basic and intrinsic similarities. This creates harmony and generosity, because doing good to others is doing good to ourselves.

When we choose to be compassionate, we are choosing to be openhearted. It creates room for vulnerability, and that is all the more reason to embody that emotion. When we are openhearted, we are living in our natural state—generosity and love are present, and gratitude is overflowing. In this state we can recognize how we are connected and can see things with a "we" focus rather than "me" focus. Being openhearted can be the act of smiling at a stranger, thinking kind thoughts about someone, wishing someone well, or being open to the possibility of connection. Live this way, and you will start to notice that many of life's unexpected and incredible moments were brought on by being openhearted, embracing surrender and trust.

JET LAG TOOL KIT
HOW TO OPEN YOUR HEART
SO YOU CAN OPEN YOUR EYES

1. **Adopt a "Be first" mindset.** Be the first to smile, say hello, or perform a kind, simple act of connection. Try this out with random strangers. Smile at someone as you pass on the sidewalk. Even if they don't smile back, I guarantee they will feel the effects of your simple kindness and it will create a ripple effect. Kindness tends to be more contagious than herpes, after all.

2. **Use discomfort as a compass for openhearted action.** Lean into the fear to take away its power and be kind to yourself if things don't go as planned. Celebrate the fact that you tried, and that you chose love over fear. It will get easier.

3. **Put your hands on your heart and breathe deeply.** This action allows you to anchor yourself and subconsciously helps you to get out of the judgemental dick mind and into your heart.

4. **Cultivate gratitude.** It's a great way to get into your heart and assist in openhearted decision-making. Make a list of things you are grateful for and truly feel the joy and appreciation for each of those things.

CHAPTER TWO
THE ART OF LETTING GO

LETTING GO 101

"And above all, watch with
glittering eyes the whole world
around you because life's greatest
secrets are always hidden
in the most unlikely places.
Those who don't believe in magic
will never find it."

ROALD DAHL

Just as those who don't believe in magic will never find it, those who attempt to control the uncontrollable will never see the beauty and grace of entering a flow state and trusting in the intentional and magnificent twists and turns of life. But of course, that is so much easier said than done.

The good news is that life is patient and persistent as hell. It continues to tirelessly offer up moments to participate in the present with enthusiasm and receptivity. The more we acknowledge those moments and choose to see and act on them, the more they will occur and become easier to spot. It all starts with being aware, releasing control, and letting go.

If you're like most people, then you've most likely spent your whole life doing the opposite, and the thought of letting go of control seems tougher than a gummer trying to eat jerky. How the heck can you continue to be safe and stay on course toward accomplishing your goals if you don't control everything?

It's a process of one firm, knowing step forward and several doubtful steps back. Every day, life presents us with countless moments to practice the art of letting go.

For years, the concept of letting go confused the shit out of me. It's one of those things that people say to do but never provide a blueprint for. I am a "set-a-goal, make-a-plan, follow-the-steps" kind of person, so the vague instructions of just "let it go" didn't really serve me. Hot damn, it was frustrating. Let it go *how*?

Well, over the last several years I have made it my Type-A mission to break this down in a way I can understand and apply to my self-structured way of life. Rather than wait until you get ass deep into this book, I wanted to offer some initial helpful tools that can be used in times of low emotional resistance. If you have had a similar experience as me, then there will be many occasions in which trying so desperately to let go ironically leads to more attempts to take control—which in turn leads to a horrible cycle of disappointment, control, and doubt. Here's what to do instead.

1. **Breathe.** Isn't it interesting that when you see or hear this word you automatically are inclined to take a deep breath?
2. **Put your hands on your heart and give thanks for three moments**. They could be big moments, little moments, funny moments, recent moments, old moments, what-the-fuck-ever moments. Just be grateful

for anything and feel it as though you are experiencing those moments in real time. Breathe deeply so that your gut expands, hold it for a few seconds, and then let it go in a long, full exhalation (what up, step one!).

3. **When negative emotions like anger, frustration, or worry show up, observe them.** Being aware of an emotion as it occurs creates separation between the emotion and the person experiencing it.

For example, let's say I lose my shit because my dog, Donut, becomes nuttier than squirrel turds during car rides and won't listen to a word I say. I put him in the very back of my Jeep and have a mesh screen separating him from the back seats to contain both him and his plethora of Golden Retriever fur. As soon as I turn the key, he can no longer hold back his excitement and begins running back and forth, left to right, over and over again. It's like Jim Carrey in *Dumb and Dumber* when he's in the van, pumping his fists like crazy, pretending to run ("It feels like you're running at an incredible rate!"). At stop lights, my car shakes from side to side. Immediately, a noise fills my head and consumes me with "all or nothing" thoughts like *Damn it, he _never_ listens. He's _never_ going to get better.* I feel the urge to blame. Others, Donut, myself. Even though most of the time he's mellow and obedient, his Jekyll and Hyde transformation in the car makes me forget about the good times. The mind quickly flies out of control, with each defensive argument attempting to justify my self-righteous reasoning. Tumble-furs—clusters of his shedding coat—escape the screen barrier and drift into my face for good measure.

On and on the mind spirals, winding up in a tormented state of suffering simply because it is out of control. This is where my focus must be centered: on training the mind and guiding it patiently and lovingly back into a mindful, calm, grateful state. So as the noise increases and tension spreads, I try to breathe and examine with curiosity how the emotion appears within my body and mind. Just be.

Watch the emotion with curiosity. Wow, I notice when the feelings of frustration amplify, they morph into anger. My shoulders tense. I furrow my brow to form a facial buttcrack between my eyes. I clench my jaw. My breathing becomes shallow. My mind starts freaking out, the thoughts becoming louder and louder. How interesting! What else is happening?

Observing your emotions and breathing deeply through them allow the emotion to pass more quickly. You must experience and acknowledge the emotion for it to move through you. If you try to shut it down, it will come back even stronger the next time. Identify it, feel it, observe it, thank it (it is teaching you, after all), and then breathe through it.

Practice these three basic steps as we move forward. Celebrate the small wins in the moments you can catch yourself and simply observe your current state.

Letting go is an art. There is no rulebook. This is one of the reasons it can be so frustrating for a goal-oriented person. Letting go feels elusive and unattainable because it does not jibe with our structured, accomplishment-oriented mindset. Fortunately, this means we can create our own strategy that works specifically for us. We get to be creative in our approach. It is our duty to examine who we are and what works for us. If we remain patient and nurturing toward ourselves during this process, it can be almost enjoyable. When we are learning something new it is easy to be harsh with ourselves. Instead, I suggest imagining yourself as a young child and expressing patience and love to that image of yourself. Be kind, loving, and compassionate.

There are so many opportunities for us to practice during our days. The key is to seek out these moments for what they really are: occasions to learn, grow, and improve. Overcome the incessant doubt that attempts to attack us as soon as we show a tiny bit of vulnerability when we are learning something new, and say "Thank you for your concern, but I got this. I want to experience this and grow." Thanking your emotions helps you remain aware that the emotion is separate from yourself, and lets you feel it rather than stifle it. Just a simple "No thank you" works, too.

PATTERNS

Each of us has lessons we must learn in this life, and until we do, we will repeatedly be presented with opportunities to learn them. Looking back on your life, you may notice a theme or pattern of events that often resulted in similar attempted lessons. Always falling into a bad relationship, never having enough money, having the same type of argument with family or friends, etc. I've noticed that the various lessons I'm meant to learn amplify in intensity the more I avoid or ignore them.

Letting go has been an interesting and persistent theme in my life. I knew it was something I needed to do, and yet I would often find myself ruminating over situations to the point of absolute frustration and self-sabotage. This was especially the case in three particular circumstances:

1. If I was in a disagreement with someone and I felt like they didn't see my point of view.
2. If I made a mistake, I would replay it constantly in my mind, sometimes learning from it but never letting it go.
3. To feel safe or happy, I felt I had to control everything, never letting go and surrendering.

Each of these were different aspects of letting go that repeated themselves throughout the decades, all centered around one main theme: surrender. Through disagreements with family members, friends, and business partners, each time the emotions involved grew in magnitude as the stakes became higher. The feeling of being wronged but not having my side heard or understood infuriated me. How could they not see my point of view? How could they think they were right?! The scenario would play out in my mind on repeat, hours of hypothetical confrontations that never resulted in anything but fleeting relief that I'd proved my point and really "showed them" while debating with myself as I drove/cooked/took a piss. I had a loop of self-justification playing constantly in my mind, nearly impossible to ignore. It was making me act in ways I was not proud of: defensive, self-righteous, compassionless, quick to anger.

When life really wants you to grasp the lesson you were meant to learn, it will act like a toddler having a full-blown shit-fit in the toy store, becoming impossible not to notice. In that moment, you have a choice. Can you take a step back to reflect on your life, see the patterns related to that lesson, and evaluate how you've dealt with it to this point? Did you avoid it? Ignore it? Play the victim? Refuse to take responsibility? Blame or judge others? Truthfully look back on the ways it has presented itself while wearing different masks over the years. Then try to look at the pattern in a new light. What were you meant to learn from it?

For me, I had to learn how to let go and take responsibility for my life. I had to figure out a strategy for being okay with not having my point of view heard and let go of the piece of me that felt so insistent on being right. Instead, I needed to look at the situation with compassion, both for the other person and for myself. Every time I reflexively thought *Fuck you very much* I would quickly replace it with *Thank you*. I was thanking the situation for giving me the opportunity to practice finding the lesson.

Life has provided me with more mistakes and unforeseen situations than I could count. I've had to learn to find the lesson in them and then, just as important, let them go. Holding onto mistakes or memories in which things went badly because I wasn't in control didn't reinforce the lesson. It just made it harder to learn fully. To truly understand the lesson, I had to let go of the situation that taught it. They were meant to be transient, but in my fear I was grasping hold of them and keeping them close. The more I did this, the more difficult it became to hear the lessons they taught.

What are the patterns in your life? Look back with curiosity at the situations that generate a negative reaction of anger, sadness, despair, or frustration. The first step to learning from them is to acknowledge them. You will find that many of them have morphed over the years into a nearly unmanageable beast. It's best to take care of it before it grows even bigger. Because life will do whatever it takes to get you to pay attention until you finally grasp the lessons you were meant to learn.

YOU GET WHAT YOU ASK FOR

In 2018, my husband Jeff and I decided it was time to pull the goalie and pump out some love nuggets. We ran our own business and had a plan to time the birth of our future baby so the due date would fall just after our company's busy season. Nearly all of our friends had gotten knocked up on the first try, much to the disappointment of the husbands who were hoping for more time to practice. We expected it would be just as easy.

Life has an ironic sense of humor, though. It tends to give us exactly what we ask for, but rarely in the way we want it.

In December 2018, I got on a kick to learn how to accept the present moment with an open heart and surrender to life instead of resisting it. I wanted to see what would happen if I stopped trying to fight reality and learned to accept it instead. That year, I naively made a New Year's resolution: learn how to let go of my constant need to control and attempt to trust in life instead.

There are few better ways to do this than to try to get pregnant. After 17 years, I went off the birth control pill and learned that aunt flow was MIA. Month after month went by without surfing the crimson wave. Each month, I walked the tightrope of hope and disappointment as I pissed on the plastic stick that would determine my fate. Hope is persistent and often irrational, and no matter how much you try to mentally prepare yourself for a negative, it feels like a left hook to the uterus every time you see your hopes denied.

After six months I went to the doctor, who performed a series of blood tests and ultrasounds and then referred me to the REI department. I quickly learned that the acronym refers to Reproductive Endocrinology and Infertility, not the cool store that sells outdoor recreational equipment. More appointments, paperwork, blood tests, and ultrasounds resulted in the doctor's determination that I was an anomaly—something a person doesn't want to be in the eyes of medical staff.

Without knowing the cause, I received a blanket diagnosis of Ovulatory Infertility from Secondary Amenorrhea. I learned a lot about female anatomy. My faded pink hospital gown was like a pair of medical assless chaps, and drafts of cold air caught me off guard as the doctor showed me plastic models of the female reproductive system. It was 7th grade sex ed all over again, except this time I was paying attention.

Ovulation is apparently a *very* important piece of the pregnancy puzzle; without it, your chances of making an oven-bun are nonexistent. The doctor recommended Clomid to kickstart follicular growth, paired with a self-injection of Ovidrel to force ovulation. The first cycle, I was on the lowest dose of Clomid. But still I over-responded, producing so many eggs that if I conceived, I would have had a litter of babies Cruella de Vil would envy. It was deemed too dangerous, so the doc said we'd try Letrozole next since it was less likely to cause over-production.

Three expensive failed cycles later, hormones all out of whack, and with disappointment levels at an all-time high, my husband and I decided to take a break from medical intervention for a couple of months. Neither of us wanted to go the IVF route, feeling like it just wasn't the right option for us. More than a year had passed since we had excitedly decided to start trying, thinking it would be fun, quick, and easy.

Infertility is interesting, though. It's the ultimate practice in learning to let go. I quickly realized that I could do everything right and pregnancy still might not happen. Medications, injections, supplements, books, articles, apps, acupuncture, abdominal massages, meditations, fertility diets and cleanses—you name it, I probably tried it. I couldn't help but question whether I was trying to force something that wasn't meant to be. Maybe I was just infertile as fuck and that was that.

If you're having difficulty conceiving, you become keenly aware of all the fertile people in your life. Babies and clever pregnancy announcements clog your Instagram feed. Strollers are absolutely everywhere. You spot baby bumps with an eagle eye of desire for something you want but can't seem to have (unless you eat a gigantic burrito).

Over the course of TTC (that's Trying to Conceive, for the uninitiated), five of my closest friends and immediate family members cautiously, almost apologetically, shared news of their pregnancies with me. I learned a lot with each announcement. First off, practice makes perfect doesn't necessarily apply here. Instead of getting easier, the more pregnancy announcements I heard, the harder it got. Each call or text felt like a swift kick to the ovaries, and was always followed by an ugly cry on the floor.

I would be consumed by an overwhelming guilt that my first reaction wasn't joy and excitement for the people I cared deeply about. The genuine happiness for them would come shortly after, but I had trouble compassionately accepting my initial response. Feeling bad about feeling bad creates a vicious cycle, and it wasn't until I accepted that it's perfectly okay to be sad for myself and happy for someone else simultaneously that I finally found some peace.

I started to be kinder to myself and honor my reactions. I noticed that when I did this, the amount of time before I felt at peace with my situation greatly improved, and I was able to share others' excitement authentically. I knew the easiest option would have been to close off to protect myself from the devastating hurt and disappointment, but there was something inside me insisting that I embrace the pain and learn to accept it without muting it.

When we experience disappointment, we have two options. We can close off and shut down, thinking we're protecting ourselves from pain by attempting to numb it, or we can choose love and experience the hurt with an open heart. The former is much easier in the short-term, but as time passes, it will lead to a bitter and lonely resentment that will harden our hearts and stifle our joy.

There's no denying that getting bad news sucks nuts. Getting crappy news while your bare ass is propped up on the crunchy paper of a doctor's examination table, feet in stirrups and fully exposed, takes it to another level entirely.

My doctor rested a kind hand on my knee and even behind her face mask, I could see that something was wrong.

"Your pregnancy isn't progressing. There's no heartbeat."

Her words felt like Bruce Lee straight blasted me right in the uterus.

I found myself in the awkward situation of feeling compelled to reassure my doctor that it was okay while literally caught with my pants down. I'm not an overly emotional woman, so I often find myself trying to comfort people as they try to comfort me. I prefer to tough it out and cope with sadness by myself, away from the sympathetic and pitying eyes of others.

So, I put on my go-to positive front, telling her everything was okay. After all, it was a good sign that I could actually get pregnant, considering I had been trying for so long. Fortunately, my face mask concealed the involuntary lip quiver that would've blown my cover. Hope evaporated the moment I saw the ultrasound screen.

Jeff was waiting in the car, since he wasn't allowed inside due to coronavirus concerns. When I walked outside, even through my mask and sunglasses, he knew. I saw his shoulders slump and concern spread across his face as soon as he saw mine.

A little over a month prior, I had pissed on a stick, unable to believe my eyes. It was positive. After a year and a half of negatives, I had stopped believing I would ever see the double lines indicating pregnancy. I gripped the pee stick with both hands, held it to my heart, and laughed out loud.

When we first started trying to get knocked up, the negatives would sit on the counter and torture me, taking my three minutes of anticipation and pinching my hope out like a flame. But after a couple of months of this, I noticed a change. I inadvertently stopped hoping. When you start to expect a negative result, it numbs the pain of disappointment. I no longer allowed myself to daydream of a future child, no longer let myself imagine what they would look like, what their nickname would be, or what it would be like to share my passion for travel with my family.

As soon as I got that positive result, everything came pouring back. Hope, joy, and excitement took over—proving it was never gone, just waiting. Jeff and I would go on walks and let our imaginations run wild, picturing the ways in which our life was about to change. We started dreaming again.

Because of my history with infertility, my doctor had me take two blood tests in week four to confirm HCG levels were rising appropriately, and, once the pregnancy was confirmed, I had my first ultrasound at six and a half weeks. My OB could only see the gestational sac and yolk sac, but no baby, which can sometimes happen if the timing is miscalculated. We scheduled a second ultrasound a week later, and although I was still hopeful, I began to mentally prepare for the worst.

It seems like no matter how much you brace for misfortune, nothing can ever fully remove the sting once it occurs. Nothing I had experienced came close to the news of a failed pregnancy after that pure elation, imagining our family coming to fruition.

My D&C surgery day began with Jeff and I wishing each other a happy anniversary, a fairly fucked up coincidence. Once again, he was not allowed into the building because of COVID restrictions, so he pulled up to the roundabout as I put on my mask, gave him a hug, and hopped out, much like a kid getting dropped off for their first day of school.

The huge waiting room was completely empty, and it felt like an eerie dream. Every other chair was taped off, and couches were pushed against the wall like a makeshift furniture fort. The nurse called my name, and I followed her to room 4, where she asked me to remove everything and put on a gown, hairnet, and sexy beige non-skid socks. When she came back, she asked where my mask was and told me it had to stay on the whole time. Apparently, taking off everything did not include my most-used accessory from the last few weeks.

The next fifteen minutes were a chaotic blur. Two rushed nurses simultaneously asked me medical history questions while hooking me up to IVs and electrodes, and then I was left to watch the wall in silence as I waited for the surgery to start.

After an hour, my doctor came in and asked how I was doing, a gentle smile behind her mask. She gave me a brief rundown of the surgery and said we'd be starting in a few minutes. A friendly, less-rushed nurse came in shortly after and said she'd be helping out. She expertly pushed my gurney through the hospital hallways, dodging corners and medical equipment like a pro. She lined me up next to the surgery table and I tried to move myself over without ass-flashing the anesthesiologist standing nearby. I could tell by the draft I felt that my attempts were in vain, and he may or may not have gotten a wink from the brown eye.

I looked around and saw cushioned leg straps resting above my head. I dreaded the thought of being knocked out cold, legs in the air under the bright fluorescent lights. As the anesthesiologist began to connect to my IV, the nurse removed my face mask before quickly replacing it with an oxygen mask.

After what felt like just a couple of minutes, I blinked my eyes open in the recovery room and was given a glass of water. I tried to drink through my mask, not realizing it was back on my face.

A nurse helped me get dressed as I clumsily tried to guide

my limbs into uncooperating clothing, my lady bits popping out of the gown like they had an exhibitionist mind of their own. I was wheeled outside, where Jeff was waiting in his truck for his wifely curbside pick-up.

The days after the surgery were a total mindfuck. Physically, I felt perfectly fine—no pain whatsoever. Everything on the outside carried on as though nothing had happened. The sun was shining, work continued as normal, and the earth continued to spin. The only tangible reminder of my D&C was my bruised arm from the IV. The external seemed like a lie, and I wished that the physical pain matched how emotionally thrashed I was.

I felt undeserving of the depression I was experiencing. I was only knowingly pregnant for a little over a month and was angry that I had let myself get so excited so quickly. But trying to reason with your feelings is nearly impossible. To recover from such heavy sadness, I had to let myself grieve without judgement from my harshest critic: myself.

I tried to be compassionate as I was slammed by tumultuous waves of grief. Anger, regret, heartbreak, and despair engulfed every aspect of my being, knocking the wind out of me, and leaving me feeling like I would never get back up to the surface.

At times, acceptance would come, and I would briefly be at peace, knowing that if I had attempted to mute the joy I'd felt after becoming pregnant it wouldn't have made this pain any easier. Instead, it would have just muted the vibrant and authentic parts of life. I knew that to feel fully was to live fully.

Still, I wanted to shut myself off from everyone and everything. But I ended up doing something completely out of character. I sent an email to a handful of close friends and family informing them of the pregnancy-turned-miscarriage and was honest about how devastated I was. I didn't sugarcoat it or comfort them as I had done with the doctor. It was raw vulnerability about a subject that was rarely discussed yet very common.

My inbox was flooded with sincere words of love and support. Some even opened up and shared intimate stories of their own miscarriages, while others dropped off care packages filled with cookies and booze. Each person expressed their empathy with such genuine kindness that I no longer felt so alone.

Unexpectedly, I felt immense gratitude and joy.

My heart was full during a time when it should have been empty, and the crushing disappointment that consumed me began to subside.

My suffering began to heal through openhearted connection with others.

As I leaned on my loved ones, I started to approach the surface. I no longer felt like I was drowning.

So many people move through life with walls built up to protect themselves from the vulnerability of being openhearted, because it could hurt. In fact, it's almost guaranteed to hurt at some point. But what most people don't realize is that the barriers we create to protect us imprison us. To acknowledge the potential for great pain or sadness if you lower your guard in the face of disappointment, and then still choose love over fear, is one of the most courageous things that people can do. And it's the only way to truly let go and live fully.

Why do we always try to fight with reality when it doesn't

meet our vision of how it should be?

Life happens. It doesn't meet our expectations and we take it personally. Rather than accept the situation for what it is, we desperately try to change it. But what happened, happened. No amount of mental MacGyver-ing will change that. The only thing we can control is the meaning we give those events and the choices we make in response. Do we choose love, or fear?

Life finds a way to give us just what we ask for via situations that may initially appear as problems. If we look closely, we can see that they are actually the opportunities we've been requesting. It's as though whenever we decide we want to change in a certain way or adopt a new habit, life will provide us with some sort of obstacle in which we can practice that very trait. It's almost as if we're being tested: How badly do we want that thing we long for? How much are we willing to overcome to get it?

So many times, we end up ignoring these opportunities for practice and yet continue to say we want the very thing those opportunities would provide. The next time a problem arises in your life, I suggest examining it with curious, even humorous eyes. What is the challenge? What have you asked for? What are you meant to learn? The answers are there. You just need to look for them.

It comes down to accepting reality with an open heart, choosing love, and letting go. By refusing to let the pain of unmet expectations embitter you, you can lean into the present moment and show up as you are. It's only then that you can experience life as it was meant to be lived—from a place of raw authenticity and wholehearted participation.

JET LAG TOOL KIT
HOW TO LET GO

The practice of letting go isn't limited to surrendering to life's events. We also face the challenge of letting go of negative reactions to situations in which we feel we've been wronged or misunderstood, or moments of regret or shame. The more emotionally charged the response, the longer it stays with us. People often say, "Just let it go!" like this is obvious or simple, or like it can easily be done just by speaking those words. That never worked for me. I would wonder *how.* What steps did I need to take to let things go fully and completely so I could be free from my mind's (illogical, exaggerated) reactions? I would tell myself to just let something go over and over again, and yet no matter how many times I tried, it would still stick with me.

In his books and courses, Michael Singer goes into great detail about the importance of letting go and how to apply this practice to your life. He explains the different ways we hold onto situations and reactions that are actually meant to be transient, and how, as a result, we suffer. We cling to things we were never meant to hold onto. Singer has several techniques for learning to let go, and below is a brief overview of some of the recommendations I've found invaluable.

1. **Replace the negative thought with a positive one.** OK, duh. This sounds so simple, and like something we all already know. The thing is, few of us actually *use* this technique when we need it most. As soon as you notice that you're having a negative reaction to something, replace that auto-response with a positive reframing of the event. For example, you're at the grocery store and in a rush, but there is a huge line of people that seems

to be moving slower than a snail race. My typical reaction would be to get impatient and frustrated. This would be a great time to catch your initial response and reframe it. Instead of listening to the negative and judgmental chatter of the mind, think to yourself, *Wow, how lucky am I that I can afford food? This extra time standing in line is a great opportunity for me to give thanks for the fact that I can afford this meal I am about to buy.* With consistent practice, your auto-response will become one of positivity and gratitude.

2. **Relax and release**. The instant you notice a negative reaction arise, whether it stems from the present moment or a memory, tell yourself to relax. Actively focus on relaxing your shoulders, jaw, stomach, heart, and thoughts. Feel everything relax. Say to yourself, *I choose to relax and release.*

Just the action of shifting your attention to relaxing and releasing creates space between the negative reaction and your seat of self (basically, you as a conscious individual). This is the first step towards detachment. When you detach from your reactions, you begin to find freedom in knowing that you are not your emotions. They are separate from you. Relax, observe the feeling with curiosity, and release it.

The more you do these things, the easier they become. With consistent effort, you'll notice that things that used to get your undies all bunched up no longer have as much power. Eventually you may find that you don't react at all. Past grudges and guilt will soften and eventually disappear, finally enabling the freedom that was meant to be yours all along.

CHAPTER THREE
BRIDGING THE GAP

FRANCE

When I was a junior in high school, I went on my first solo travel adventure. It was a test of every part of me. I applied to participate in a study abroad program through American Field Service (AFS) in hopes of going to Australia for six months. I was accepted, but two months prior to my departure I was told that there were no longer enough host families down under, so I got to choose between the other available countries: Italy, Venezuela, or France. My high school didn't offer Italian as a foreign language, and Venezuela was in a turbulent political state at that time. So, I decided on the land of baguettes and berets. I quickly switched from Spanish class to French to cram in as much as I could before going; by the time I left, I could sing French children's songs, count to ten, and say *bonjour*. Not exactly well-prepared, but it was better than nothing.

AFS provided me with a packet of information about the family I would live with in Bourges—a dad, mom, an eighteen-year-old son who had studied in New York the year prior, and a fifteen-year-old daughter. The packet contained cultural information, tips for combatting culture shock, and advice for being a successful representative of the United States. Then, before I knew it, I was pulling up to San Francisco International Airport with my mom, dad, sister, and three best friends. I said goodbye, and as I walked through security and down the terminal hall, I kept looking back to see them huddled together, waving and smiling. Once I turned the corner and they were out of sight, the reality of the situation hit me.

I felt a confused, blurred wave of excitement and fear. I was on my own. I was seventeen years old and going to another country where I didn't know a soul, didn't know the language, didn't know shit. It was an absolutely terrifying thrill.

AFS held a two-day orientation in New York to prepare the program participants for life abroad. We practiced initial introductions with our future families, acted out different situations and challenges we might face, and learned what life and high school would be like in France. I quickly learned that I was the worst at French. Most of the other students had at least a full year of the language, and many had more than that. I desperately scribbled notes on pronunciation for basic phrases and learned how to say, "My name is Kat" and "I'm from California."

My nerves were rising with every moment, my mental soundtrack playing *What the fuck did I get myself into?* on repeat. I have always been an incredibly shy person, and painfully so as a little kid. I would whisper what I had to say to my dad when we were at my grandparents' house for the holidays, too scared to speak in front of relatives. But I've also always been driven to overcome what scares me. A glutton for discomfort, growth, and achievement. Plus, I had always dreamed of being an explorer, from the time I was a little girl. So, the equation that presented itself as I prepared to go to France was: One super shy girl plus a passion and deep curiosity for travel equals someone going halfway across the globe feeling terrified yet fully alive.

After a long, sleepless flight we landed in Paris, then dispersed via train to our final destinations for the next six months. I boarded the train to Bourges, a centrally located city known for its timbered houses, cobblestone streets, and gothic Cathedral. When I arrived, a man and his teenaged son greeted me in French. After realizing how little I knew, the boy helped me out by switching to English. I'd brought gifts for everyone, and when I asked where the daughter and mom were, I learned that they had divorced a couple of years prior and that I would be living with the two guys. That probably would have been good to know beforehand…just sayin'. But one of the things we'd learned at the orientation was that things are not bad, just different, and it is crucial to learn to go with the flow and accept the differences between our expectations and reality. It was a lesson in surrender at a very young age.

The first couple of weeks were hugely overwhelming. My brain grew exhausted trying to sort out an entirely new vocabulary. I tried my best to follow along in my classes, but some of the teachers were brutal. My English teacher used me as an example of the ways in which American English was not proper and should not be used by my classmates. She frequently made students cry: announcing the worst test score in the class, having that student stand before the room as they took a verbal beating. The time I was berated for not knowing the difference between *who* and *whom* will forever be etched into my mind. On the positive side, cafeteria lunches in France are some of the best ever. The excellence of French cuisine is a stereotype that is one hundred percent accurate. The lunch lady served beef bourguignon and chocolate soufflé instead of sloppy joe's, extra sloppy for ya.

Living with two dudes was better than I expected in some

ways—and worse in others. The boy ended up being my ally. The dad did things I excused by writing them off as evidence of a slightly fucked up French sense of humor, but I later realized it was less humor and more temper. I carried a little notebook and pen everywhere I went so I could jot down words I didn't know or record things I learned (which was pretty much everything). The dad was obsessed with me always having my notebook. He spoke to me in French, and when I didn't remember something he had already told me he would scream, red in the face, *OÙ EST TON CAHIER?! Je te l'ai déjà dit!!* (Where is your notebook?! I already told you this!!). The boy would try to stand up for me and say how hard it was to remember everything when I was being bombarded by so much new information. The dad, depending on his mood, would either apologize or call me pathetic and unable to learn.

One time, two months in, the dad and I were in the kitchen preparing dinner and I asked what a word meant. I *gasp* did not have my notebook since I was cooking, so he grabbed the knife he was using to cut veggies and held it about two inches from my chest as he screamed, *"OÙ EST TON CAHIER?!"* Then, after seeing my look of absolute *What-the-Fuck?!*, he laughed and lowered the knife. What the fuck, indeed.

I tried to push through, chalking the difficulties up to the cultural differences we trained for during orientation. But we'd never covered irate host fathers obsessed with notebooks. After talking with some fellow AFSers and hearing how much they loved their host families, I realized my situation was a little abnormal. No other girl was living in a home without other women. Everyone's host families were encouraging and patient as they learned French. I decided to reach out to the regional coordinator at AFS to switch families. They agreed to move me, and the two weeks it took to find a new family were some of the longest and most awkward of my life. I was stuck living with people who knew I didn't want to live with them anymore. Fortunately, the dad mostly gave me the silent treatment or spewed the occasional under-the-breath comment for the remainder of my stay.

Eventually they found me a new family in Esvres, a small town about thirty minutes from the city of Tours and a couple hours from Bourges. I went to school in Tours, and it was a huge improvement. The English and French teachers both gave me French-as-a-second-language activities and homework. The food was fantastic, and the kids were incredibly kind and welcoming. My new host family was nice but had some quirks. There was a dad, a mom, an eighteen-year-old boy, and an eight-year-old boy. They had twin sixteen-year-old daughters who were studying abroad in Germany, so I got to stay in their room. There was just one bathtub in the home, and the door to that bathroom did not lock, so you had to inform everyone if you were going to bathe so nobody walked in. One of the aforementioned "quirks" was that the host dad would conveniently water his plants just outside the frosted glass bathroom window every time I made my shower-time announcement. *Très pervy.* But, on the upside, the host mom taught me how to cook French food and gave me lots of Nutella, and the family never screamed at me about not knowing what something meant. A fair trade.

Total submersion in a new culture was an incredible way

to learn. After a few months, my dreams went from being in English, to *Franglais*, to French, and I remember one day on the drive to Tours I realized that I had understood everything that was being said on the talk-radio show my host mom was listening to. For the most part, making friends was easy, especially because I was from California. This was 2003, a time when there was a lot of tension between the United States and France because of the Iraq War. I remember hearing that the U.S. wanted to spite France by changing the name of our dietary staple, French fries, to Freedom Fries. My poor friend Beth had a rough time with first impressions, being from Idaho, a place perceived by our classmates to be an unknown potato state somewhere in the middle of the country. I, however, was lucky. Kat from California was a curiosity. *Do you know Brad Pitt? Do you surf every day? Do you go to school in a swimsuit? Are you a cheerleader?* The perception of California was much different from the perception of the United States as a whole, and it worked in my favor, making up for my lack of French skills.

The months went by quickly, and before I knew it, the school year was ending and I was about to head home. My time in France was a blend of awesome times and difficult moments, and the experience taught me an invaluable lesson. Pushing myself far past my comfort zone was the best way to grow and reach my potential.

Discomfort is one of the greatest gifts a person can give themselves. It's a fantastic way to get to know who you really are and what you're capable of. There were times in France when I felt incredibly lonely and defeated, but eventually I learned to recognize that in those moments of despair, I always had myself to depend on.

In moments of isolation and loneliness, when you crave compassion and support but can't find it externally, you must create it from within. Doing so will transform loneliness to solitude, and teach you that you are capable of more than you realize. That you are more than enough. That you will overcome. That you're resilient, and even if you are feeling down, you can get up and keep going. When you push through doubt and trust in your ability, your whole life transforms into a fascinating journey of unbridled potential just waiting to be exposed.

PURPOSE

What am I meant to be doing with my life? Am I on the right track? Why am I here? What is my purpose? These questions have been at the forefront of human thought for thousands of years. Mulled over by great philosophers and average Joes alike, these questions have been top of mind for most of us as we question whether we are doing what we are meant to be doing. We are told to live in a state of paradox: plan for the long-term, but live as if you'll croak tomorrow. We become accustomed to the routines of our lives and time passes in the background, only acknowledged when we glance at our calendars and are shocked that the year is almost over. One moment you are finishing school, questioning your next move, and the next, you are looking back on decades that seemed to drift by without your noticing.

I knew from a young age what my passion was. Travel consumed my thoughts. When my mom asked what I wanted for my third birthday I requested a globe piggy bank. My first solo trip at seventeen was incredibly challenging but absolutely invigorating. To go someplace halfway across the world where I didn't know a soul and create a new life was fascinating. Through even the most difficult situations, I felt at home in my discomfort and more alive than ever. I was hooked.

In college, I got the opportunity to study abroad in Spain for a year, and a couple of years after graduating I went on a six-month solo trip to South America. Most of my life had been spent wondering if I was doing what I was meant to be, and whether I was on the right track.

When I travel, it's one of the only times I feel absolute conviction that I am exactly where I should be, doing exactly what I should be doing. I know how to surrender and find the humor in life's unexpected events. The characteristics I grasp for in daily life naturally flow through me. I feel alive and wild and true to my core. And yet, I always return and continue my "real life."

After a trip, I settle into my routine of work, life, being a friend, wife, dog mom, and so on, saving for the next travel opportunity. If I let too much time pass between trips, I notice a depletion of my spirit. It begins with a deep nostalgia and transforms into a desperate longing for the adventure of far-off lands that will offer me assurance of my purpose and passion. Travel recharges my soul.

I've often wondered if I could somehow bridge the gap between "Travel Me" and "Domestic Me." I don't know if I have ever felt that same sense of knowing and assuredness when I wasn't traveling, and it's led me to many moments of doubt and frustration. When I travel, I feel like the best parts of me radiate effortlessly, like I possess all the characteristics I strive to embody. Letting go of control, being openhearted, seeing the gift or lesson in each situation, finding the generosity, humor, gratitude, and joy: It all happens with ease when I'm in a new environment.

As much as I would like to just travel forever, I have somewhat contradictory goals. I long to keep a homebase with my husband, family, and friends, and to start a family of my own. I believe that rather than making this situation an either/or proposition, it's possible for me to make it a both/and. So often our first instinct is to limit our options to make a decision. If we can change our mindset to one of abundance and acknowledge the possibility of actually having it all, we may realize that the greatest limits we face are the ones we set for ourselves.

I must recognize that I *do* know how to live in a way that is consistent with my values of surrender, acceptance, and openness. I know I can do this, since I have proven that during my travels it is a natural piece of who I am. One of my lessons in this life is to learn to capture that joy and acceptance for the present moment in every situation, whether I am in the middle of a bustling Moroccan bazaar or waiting in line at the store while Air Supply plays on loudspeakers under fluorescent lighting.

This involves trusting that I'm exactly where I'm meant to be, accepting the reality of the moment and pushing aside my perceptions of how it should be. *Should* does not matter. *Should* is not reality. So, I've had to stop *should*ing all over myself. The moment, regardless of how much we like or dislike it, is reality. I believe if we can learn to accept the present moment for what it is, then we will be able to find a sense of peace and certainty that we are right on track. We can find the beauty in the mundane and see the miracle in the ordinary. We can begin to slow time by appreciating the familiar rather than just focusing on future travels or upcoming exciting events.

When I travel, I tend to see everything as new and view what would typically be considered mundane with fresh eyes eager to find the adventure. To apply that same sense of wonder and awe to all moments, traveling or not, would be the greatest accomplishment in appreciating all that is. It would trigger a chain reaction of stacked gratitude.

If you are questioning what you are meant to be doing in this life, it can feel like you are wasting time. A feeling of desperate urgency can consume you. Don't fall into the trap of scarcity-based thinking. If you don't have a clearly defined passion for any one thing, it can be helpful to dig deeper into anything that piques your curiosity. Focus on the situations that lit you up in the past.

- When were the moments in your life when you felt most alive?
- What was happening?
- Where were you and who were you with?
- What did it feel like?
- Is it possible to recreate those moments, or more importantly, the feelings those moments produced?

To figure out what the hell you're meant to be doing in this short-yet-long life, let's explore something I call the Triad of Purpose. It contains three forces that will catapult your awareness: openminded curiosity, drive, and surrender/trust. If you go about your day attempting to balance these factors, the path you are meant to walk will begin to reveal itself. By adopting an openminded view through genuine curiosity, you will allow yourself to be receptive to unforeseen opportunities for growth. By setting goals and giving yourself the gift of dreaming big, you will be able to take the action necessary to achieve. By surrendering to the reality of the moment while trusting in life, synchronicities will lead you on your journey.

If you place too much emphasis on any one of the three areas of the triad, the balance will be out of whack, hindering your progress. For example, too much drive disables you from seeing the nearly hidden mile-markers of serendipity or seemingly unrelated opportunities that have the potential to guide you. Being too hard-set on just one way to achieve a goal can make you miss the countless other ways of accomplishing it. Too much surrender, on the other hand, can prevent you from acting or taking one hundred percent responsibility for your life. Too much curiosity can keep you from moving forward toward a goal. Instead of taking you on a slight detour, it can take you in the opposite direction and place you in analysis paralysis. A balance of the triad's components is what lets them work their magic.

If you move through life actively focused on learning and growing as much as you can, you will become more fulfilled. Progress is happiness, and any time you improve your knowledge or skillset, you are contributing to that progress. I'm not strictly talking about expanding your knowledge in an academic way, but through personal development. The pursuit of becoming your best self is a lifelong process. There is always room for more growth. Rather than feeling overwhelmed by this never-ending challenge, try to see it as an opportunity for guaranteed happiness. The pursuit of progress is in fact the pursuit of happiness. By applying gratitude to the pursuit, you can give yourself the gift of unbridled joy. Gratitude cultivates joy. Happiness can be fleeting in that we often think we've found it by getting something we want, but once we get it, we're forced to chase that feeling by going after some other desire. By practicing gratitude, you can create joy for what you already have.

We all want to feel a sense of purpose. We want to know that we are living a life of meaning. Let's focus on amplifying moments of aliveness by being present in whatever situation is unfolding. That can be as simple as saying thank you for whatever is in front of you. Accept what *is* with grace and gratitude, and trust that it's happening for you and as it should.

There are going to be times when you don't feel like being your best self or seeing the good. During those moments, you must act the way you want to feel. "Fake it 'til you make it" is a strategy that can work wonders in so many aspects of life. Whether it's for a job you eventually want to get or a new outlook or belief you would like to embody, if you begin with acting or feeling that way, you'll eventually become what you're "faking."

Take happiness, for example. If you really want to be happy, the way to kickstart the process is to change your actions and emotions to match those of a happy person. How would a happy person act? What would they look like? What would they say, do, or think? A happy person would smile, keep their head up, laugh, be cheerful and see the good in a situation. They would probably not be slumped over, eyes down and closed off. Instead, they'd stand or sit up straight with a good, confident posture and their chin up. How would a happy person react or respond to a situation? Would they choose to see the negative or the positive? How would they interact with others? If you begin to embody the emotions and actions of the characteristics you desire, you will, in fact, do just that.

Regardless of whether you know why you are here and what you are meant to be doing, participating with the present moment from a place of love and acceptance ensures a fulfilled life. Each day we encounter infinite situations that call upon us to act. If you see every moment as an opportunity to actively participate in it and uplift the situation by showing up fully and authentically, then you've given it your all. This involves being openhearted and not closing off or shutting down during life's many shitstorms. To acknowledge the difficulty and stand firmly in your commitment to uplift the moment in any way you can, even if that just means looking for the silver lining, then you will be able to look back on a life well-lived.

JET LAG TOOL KIT
HOW TO FIND YOUR JOY

1. **Live your life with a focus on the Triad of Purpose: openminded curiosity, drive, and surrender/trust**. Just as you would rebalance your investment portfolio if part of it was not serving you, dedicate time each week to reflect on whether you are placing too much emphasis on any one aspect of the triad.

2. **Utilize your tool kit of gratitude, continuous learning/growth, and participation through love.** Live fully by pursuing never-ending growth and actively participating in the moment in front of you and do so from a place of love and contribution.

3. **When bad shit happens, actively look for the lesson, the gift, or the humor.** Get out of your beautiful, albeit slightly batshit crazy, mind and into your heart.

CHAPTER FOUR
PERFECTLY IMPERFECT

THE IMPOSSIBLE STANDARD

For most of my life, I chased perfection. At a young age I got the fucked-up idea in my head that to be loved I had to be perfect. I felt that if I didn't do something perfectly then it was a failure. It's bonkers how much this belief controlled my life. I limited myself, held parts of my personality back, and was harsh with myself when I fell short of my super high standards. Now, part of this belief did have an upside that served me, which is why I allowed it to dictate how I behaved for so long. The belief that perfection was obtainable and necessary drove me to push myself towards achievement and attempt to become the best version of myself.

It wasn't until I attended a Tony Robbins event that I became aware of how much I valued perfection—and learned that it is in fact one of the *lowest* standards a person can have for themselves, since perfection in people does not exist. My mind was blown like a back-alley BJ. I was trying to hold myself to an impossible standard, convincing myself I could not be loved unless I was perfect, which, again, was impossible. How messed up and ass-backwards is that? The irony is that I have always admired and valued authenticity and tried hard to be true to who I am, letting my genuine self shine through. What I realized is that to be truly authentic I had to give up the notion of perfection. It did not allow for me to learn or grow as much as I could, because the fear of not being perceived as perfect prevented me from trying. If I did make a mistake, I would replay it in my mind until it became etched into my memory like a scar. Sometimes, I even obsessed over hypothetical mistakes I hadn't even made yet.

For example, my eighty-pound Golden Retriever, Donut, is basically a big furry goofball. I would walk him through the park and imagine letting him off leash to run around and play, but foreboding would interrupt the peaceful reverie. In my daydream, he would chase after a squirrel (or whatever else would captivate the attention of my highly distractible Golden ham) and run into traffic. Death and guilt were surely imminent, with despair, shame, and a closed heart to follow. I kept his leash firmly attached to his collar as we continued our safe, boring stroll. Occasionally, the awful what-if would pop back into my head and I would shudder, full of guilt for a mistake I had only imagined making.

What the actual fuck?! I let a hypothetical mistake that would have been outside my control take the reins to my mind and prevent what could have been a really nice situation. Fear of making a mistake or failing has kept countless moments of wholehearted living from happening—potential moments of joy or growth, stamped out before they had the chance to exist.

Perfection kept me from living fully. But guess what? A fully lived live is imperfect in the best way possible. Perfection kept me from trying and "failing," which could have resulted in invaluable lessons that made me a better person. Perfection led me to close my heart instead of embracing the raw vulnerability that occurs when we expose our authentic selves. When I finally realized how destructive the goal of perfection had been in my life, I drew a line in the sand. *No más, amigo*. To chase perfection is to refuse to live fully, to refuse to learn or grow.

With that realization, I chose to be authentic. I chose to value growth and learning. I chose to look like a total ass on occasion for the sake of trying something new and taking a risk. It ended up not being that bad. After all, some people like asses.

I decided that failure was not what I'd thought it was. Failure was not trying. Failure was not learning. Failure was not growing. Failure was limiting my being. And any time I tried something, gave it my all, learned from my mistakes, or was able to find the humor, it was a success. I decided that to be authentic, I had to embrace my whole self and love and appreciate its perfect imperfection. My new goal was to be unapologetically authentic and to be compassionate with myself when things didn't go as planned. I would much rather be seen and loved for who I truly am than to put on a false front in hopes of acceptance. The strongest connections are those formed through mutual authenticity and vulnerability.

Now, even though that line in the sand was deep and drawn with intensity, the winds and waves of life are inevitable and can erode your initial resolve. When I revert to old patterns of perfection-chasing and fall short of whatever standard I've set, I remind myself to be compassionate and find the humor. I think of my new definition of failure: not trying. Did I try? Did I do my best? Did I learn? I can be kind and remind myself with patience and love that I now answer to a different set of beliefs about what it means to succeed and fail.

REDEFINING FAILURE

"You may encounter many defeats,
but you must not be defeated.
In fact, it may be necessary
to encounter the defeats,
so you can know who you are,
what you can rise from,
how you can still come out of it."

MAYA ANGELOU

Failure can be viewed in many ways. Depending on the thickness of your skin and the strength of your conviction, it can feed your hunger or shatter your momentum, leaving you in a wake of disappointment and shame. Fearing failure or rejection is one of the most common ways we limit ourselves. If we take it personally, hearing *no* can deflate and defeat us. It takes vulnerability and courage to put yourself out there and try. You risk hurt, disappointment, shame, and pain. Which is why, after being burned by rejection or failure a time or two, many people stop trying at all. It's safer. It hurts less. But by taking the safer, more commonly tread path, you guarantee yourself a safe life of mediocrity. Sounds depressing and boring as hell, and yet that is how most people go about their lives.

To achieve greatness, you must experience countless

rejections and failures. The two go hand in hand. Think of the most successful and fulfilled people you can, alive or dead. Many times, super successful people are categorized as overnight successes. People tend to think everything just magically came together for them in an instant without hardship or rejection. If you look more closely, though, you will see that to be an "overnight success" those people put years, sometimes decades, toward their goal, trying, failing, and trying again until it finally worked. A common trait of the most successful people is conviction. They have grit. They do whatever it takes. When they fall, they get back up. Resilience is a habit they practice consistently. Failure is appreciated because they see it as an opportunity to learn and improve. Every *no* takes them one step closer to the *yes* they want.

Back when I was so focused on perfection, I had huge dreams: create a thriving business, travel the world, write a book, live life fully and joyfully. What I realized is that if I wanted to turn those dreams into reality, I had to accept that achieving them would involve inevitable failures and rejection. They are part of the gig. The first step was to recognize that the pain from failure was worth the possibility of accomplishing my dreams. I wanted to live a life of excellence, and to do that I had to take risks. I had to get into the arena and away from the safety of the sidelines.

My first job out of college was at a solar company where I worked doing marketing and PR. I counted down the minutes every day until 5:00pm when I could leave. The pay was fitting for someone fresh out of college with zero experience, which made me live very frugally (a necessity, considering

I was renting in the notoriously costly Bay Area). The tasks were mindless and unimportant. It was like trying to stop the Titanic from leaking with a butt plug. Everyone knew we were going down, yet we all just kept going with our time-consuming tasks. To put in the hours was more important than working strategically and efficiently. The processes were in place to be followed, not improved.

Each day, I arrived at 8:00am and walked to the large back office building with no windows, just bright florescent lights and endless rows of stuffy cubicles. The soundtrack of the workday was the constant clacking of keyboards and the occasional cough or sneeze from someone hidden behind a nearby gray wall. I was miserable. But I was lucky. I had gotten a job in 2010, a time when jobs were few and far between. I had crappy bronze handcuffs on and didn't want to quit for fear of being unable to find another pair. So, I just kept showing up and putting in the time while I dreamt of a life of freedom, wealth, and being my own boss. Then, after about a year, the company went under. I was stoked. My crap-cuffs were released!

That experience taught me something invaluable. So many of us choose the safe route of a secure job we aren't passionate about, one that merely pays the bills. We hold onto it no matter how miserable we are because we think it's less likely to fail us than if we tried something more uncommon. But as we've seen throughout history, the secure job is rarely as secure as we think. Recessions, mass layoffs, financial meltdowns, natural disasters—there are countless external forces at play that can cause us to lose everything, including that seemingly safe job we depend on so much. What I realized is that we can always fail at the thing we don't want to do, so we might as well try for that dream and risk failure for something we believe in.

Within six months of the layoff, two friends, my boyfriend (now husband), and I decided to start our own website design and development business. I was twenty-five. I learned to code by using free online resources and courses, and we grew the business so we could support ourselves and pay the bills. We weren't rich, but we were free. We designed our business around accomplishment rather than time. The goal was to get projects done, and it didn't matter when as long as it was done on time and exceptionally well. This enabled us to create processes focused on efficiency and productivity rather than just putting in the hours for the sake of working a 9 to 5. It gave me the freedom to pursue my passion of travel and the flexibility to live life on my terms.

After seven years, my husband Jeff and I decided to take another leap of faith and leave that business to pursue one helmed by just him and me. We decided to focus on different types of projects, placing more of an emphasis on creating self-branded services and web products that would enable us to achieve some really huge dreams. We had perceived safety in our first business. We had a system in place that generated enough income to cover our expenses, and things were comfortable enough. But we were hungry. We knew that to achieve what we truly wanted, we had to let go of the safety and embrace the risk.

In January 2018, we launched our husband-and-wife

venture, Alpine Design. Both of us had second jobs to supplement the insane expenses associated with living in Silicon Valley, but we knew that if we were "starving" and focused only on Alpine Design, we would not have the freedom or flexibility to strategically build our business's foundation. Hungry was better. Jeff would wake up at 4:45 every morning to work his 5:00–9:00, before heading to his second job, his 9:00–5:00. I focused on Alpine as my full-time gig, then helped manage my father's vacation rental company part-time. We would have dinner, then put in about three hours more on Alpine. We were hustling!

Our dream was to build up Alpine Design enough that we could leave our second jobs and focus fully on our business. We wanted to create helpful tools and products that would improve our clients' businesses and provide us with the lifestyle we craved. We dreamed of moving to Lake Tahoe and working from our home office overlooking the woods. This dream was worth the hustle. To prevent burn out, the "why" needed to be relevant and strong. We knew that the uncommon lifestyle we desired required an uncommon work ethic and drive. It required putting in the hours, being resilient, and acknowledging the risk of failure but going for it anyway. If we did our best, if we gave it our all, if we learned from our mistakes, and if we kept our sense of humor, then we had in fact succeeded. Our "why" acted as our fuel.

In early 2020, just before the pandemic, we visited Lake Tahoe, walking in the woods and playing out our usual conversation about how amazing it would be to live there. And then we asked ourselves two profound and important questions: What the fuck are we waiting for? and Why the fuck not? Some half-baked, fear-based excuses showed up, but then we dug deeper. Were those really reasons to postpone what we genuinely wanted? Could we make it work if we really tried? We realized that not only was it possible, but we couldn't think of a good reason not to pull the trigger. We looked up an agent and the next weekend checked out seven houses in the area. When we parked in front of the second to last place, we both knew it was the one. It was a full-body *fuck yes*. So, we placed an offer that night, it was accepted within the hour, and we moved in sixty days later.

Every day since, Jeff and I have felt disbelief and total gratitude that in the woods that day we finally decided it was time to shit or get off the pot. Sometimes the key to action simply comes down to adopting a *Fuck it, let's go for it* attitude.

Chances are there is a voice inside you that speaks of a dream you have but have discredited and buried out of fear. Maybe it's to start your own business, become a singer, write a book, become an athlete, or do stand-up comedy. Every one of us was born with a unique set of gifts given to us to help us achieve our dream and contribute to the world. Each of our experiences have shaped us so we are able to rise to that calling. The first step is to listen to the voice inside. Let it speak and be heard. Even if the dream coming true seems unlikely, it doesn't mean it is impossible. Remember, there is always a great chance that you can fail at what you don't like, so you might as well try for what you love.

If you've buried that voice within you so much that you can no longer hear it, then just follow your curiosities. They will lead you to your dreams. And as you pursue the uncommon life, just remember that each time you experience a *no*, it is taking you one step closer to the *yes* you want. To get to the *yes*, you *must* try again. Learn from the rejection and keep going. Be unstoppable in your drive. Commit to achieving your goal. Improve with each "failure," let it go, then try again. If you give up, there is zero chance that you will achieve what you want. If you try, you plant the seed of possibility. Good things may come to those who wait, but a life of greatness comes to those who hustle.

Take the risk. Allow yourself the opportunity to live the life of wonder you were born to live. Be committed to using your full potential to achieve your dreams. Break free from the limitations you have set for yourself. You create the rules of your life. All you have to do is take one step after another, no matter how small. It gets you that much closer to the life you desire. You will face pain. You will get rejected. You will experience self-doubt. It will be hard, and you'll want to give up. Don't stop. Just keep going. If you do, I promise you, it will be worth it.

JET LAG TOOL KIT
HOW TO TELL
PERFECTION TO SUCK IT

1. **Take a big-ass breath.**
2. **Think to yourself:** Thank you for trying to protect me from disappointment or shame, but I no longer need you to do that. I no longer value perfection. Instead, I value authenticity and growth, and I accept myself and all my awesome imperfections.
3. **If you made a mistake or did not achieve the "perfect" results you were hoping for, ask yourself:**
   - Did I try?
   - Did I do the best I could at the time?
   - Did I learn anything?
4. **Let. It. Go.**

CHAPTER FIVE
AUTHENTICITY

THE REAL YOU

"To avoid criticism, say nothing,
do nothing, be nothing."

ELBERT HUBBARD

In addition to my perfection-chasing, I used to be a chronic worrier about what other people thought of me. I was a people-pleaser. I tried to be agreeable, avoid conflict, shape and bend who I was so I would be liked and accepted. I was so caught up in my head that self-doubt reigned in any new social interaction. Shyness consumed and debilitated me. I would default into the nice, smiling, pleasant version of myself in hopes of being welcomed by the group. Eventually, luckily, after enough time with the same people, relationships would morph from acquaintanceships to friendships, and I would feel comfortable enough to show who I really was: a foul-mouthed slightly pervy weirdo goofball. Until I removed my false mask, acceptance could not transform into belonging.

The desire to belong has been misconstrued as a need to be accepted. To be accepted, we often try to limit our being so we can fit in with the group. We interpret not being accepted as a personal attack on who we are and whether we are "enough." As a result, we hide our authentic selves out of fear. We crave belonging, but to belong we must be authentic. To belong is to show who you really are and be loved for it. For all my people-pleasers out there, trust me, this is so very worth it.

When we acknowledge our authenticity and live in a manner that is true to who we are, we are able to be alone with ourselves in peace. We come into this world unapologetically authentic: crying, pooping our pants, knowing what we want and need, and doing whatever it takes to get it. We're all born with a unique combination of strengths, weaknesses, and gifts. As we begin to grow older and learn how to live in a way that is congruent with societal norms, we often lose sight of who we are at our core. During the process of maturing, we tend to forget a key component to our wellbeing. In our efforts to be loved and accepted we often sacrifice our authenticity.

Don't get me wrong, it is crucial that we learn not to poop our pants. But I feel like so much of our life is spent trying to get back to what we already knew coming into this world. The process of living is to forget the wisdom naturally ingrained in us, and then to relearn it through life experience. By letting go of all that keeps us from who we really are, we can learn to use our unique gifts to courageously accept ourselves fully and liberate our authentic selves.

We become accustomed to living a certain way and grow comfortable. Letting go of the parts of ourselves that no longer serve us involves changing things up, which tends to kick our comfortable self into high alert and resistance. *Why change when we are doing just fine?* it may ask. But who wants to be "just fine?" Life has the potential to be fuckin' rad. By limiting ourselves to "just fine" we prevent ourselves from living life as it was meant to be lived, which is fully. Doing so involves acknowledging the risk of potential hurt or pain and choosing to be vulnerable, pushing forward regardless of our aversion to suffering.

To live an outstanding life, we must break out of the comforts of our daily lives. We need to be vulnerable enough to lean into fear and go for it. Discomfort guides us to growth. Through continuous growth we can make progress toward becoming our best self. By committing to a life of constant growth we find ourselves in situations that take us beyond ourselves, beyond our comfort zone. It is in these moments of discomfort that the magic happens. It is worth the scrapes and bruises gathered from the experience of living a full life. To discard the inauthentic is to let go of the habits and beliefs that have led to our comfortable, just-fine lifestyle and instead completely commit to going through life with intensity and desire for becoming the greatest version of ourselves.

Every one of our personal experiences is an important piece of our life's puzzle. The problems, hardships, suffering and pain—they have all been for a purpose, for our greatest good and growth. Each moment adds to our repertoire, making us who we are. With each experience we become more prepared for the next, whether or not we actively reflect on its lesson. When we take the time to examine what can be learned from an experience, its benefits grow tenfold. Often, we regard life's discomforts as emotional wedgies, deciding only that we want less of those moments and more of the ones that feel good. Few look back to reflect on how each of those seemingly negative experiences were necessary for positive change and growth.

As we pause to reflect on our life's experiences and the winding route that's led us to where we are, we may notice that much of what we said or did was a habitual response due to our conditioning rather than an active choice. Humans are a highly adaptive species that looks for commonalities and consistencies to gain a sense of certainty. We create habits without even realizing it, unintentionally activating asshole-autopilot mode. Our upbringing creates a foundation for our belief system, telling us how to survive, receive love, and interact with others. As we grow, we do the best we can to avoid pain and pursue pleasure—the principle that guides most of our conscious and unconscious decisions.

What I propose is that today you do two things:

1. Reflect on your own asshole-autopilot responses to life.
2. Unlearn the habits that take you away from your authentic self and no longer serve you.

The act of unlearning is a willful process that requires trust and awareness. You will be surprised to find how many of your thoughts and actions occur unconsciously—your mind and body's way of making life easier for you. Its intent was never malicious. Rather, this unconsciousness was an attempt to keep you safe, minimizing pain as much as possible. But here's the kicker: What if the pain is an important part of your growth and should not be avoided? It may seem counterintuitive, but this concept is not as cut-and-dry as Pain = Bad and Pleasure = Good. Instead, Pain + Pleasure = A Deeper Life. So, we must redefine the way we react to, and find meaning in, pain and discomfort.

When events occur that prompt pain or suffering, that response is our first cue to pause and pay attention. Rather than trying to resist the negative responses as quickly as possible, we should let ourselves feel them fully. When we acknowledge pain, we begin to accept it as reality. So much of our suffering comes from resisting that reality. We get upset because what's happened isn't in line with what we wanted, and we decide this means it's wrong or bad. Your opinion of an event is based on your life's accumulation of experiences, upbringing, and attitude. And that accumulation is different for everyone. So, one experience may be viewed as a gift for one person and a goatfuck for another. The thing is, your reaction is really just an autopilot opinion formed based on your unconscious responses. It often has nothing to do with reality itself.

What happened, happened. What is, is. What will be, will be. That which is directly in front of you is reality. Your opinion of it does not change what took place, it just changes your perception of that event. An opinion is your mind's attempt to change the unchangeable. It's time to stop and recognize how bananas this is! You're moving through life, driving yourself nuts because your opinion isn't in line with reality.

Instead, we need to let go and relearn how to react to life. To drop the habits that have driven us so far away from our natural-born inner wisdom that we hardly recognize our genuine selves. Instead, let's take a stand and take control of our mind. We can begin by seeing reality as it is. Something that has occurred. A moment that has happened that we have no control over because it is done. We can begin by practicing acceptance.

When something happens, recognize that your opinion of it does not change the nature of the event or the fact that it occurred. Instead, shape your opinion of that event based on what you stand to learn. Adopt the view that every moment in life is an opportunity to grow and become a better person. Each event provides us with a choice. To choose growth over opinionated inaction. To choose to break the habit of resistance and accept what has happened, learn from it, and be grateful for it. It happened because it was meant to. There is a lesson you are meant to learn from it. I'm not saying that if someone is taking advantage of you or doing you harm, you should figuratively drop the soap and passively take it. Instead, accept reality and then take an action rooted in integrity.

By shaking up our responses we can begin to use reflection as a means of reaction. Use the following questions to create a space between reality and your habitual response.

- Why do I feel angry or sad about this?
- Why does this make me feel happy or good?
- What does this emotion feel like physically?
- What is this moment trying to teach me?
- What is the gift or the benefit?

Reflection bridges the gap between reality and acceptance. It provides us with the opportunity to actively choose our response regardless of our conditioning. Reflection enables us to unravel years of habitual reactions and take control of our attitude and our view of reality. As we reflect, we may feel inclined to pass judgement both on ourselves and on others. Avoid the temptation. Instead, tap into compassion and patience. Judgement is the mind's way of placing blame rather than practicing acceptance. Eliminate that option. Own your shit. If you trust that everything is happening exactly as it should, there is no room for judgement.

As we become accustomed to acceptance and reflection as our primary response to the present moment, we notice how much of what we do, say, and think is automatic and how little of these automatic thoughts serve our greatest good. Over the years we have stifled who we really are to gain acceptance or love. Through reflection and acceptance, we can slowly unveil our authentic self and acknowledge and appreciate the inner wisdom that has been within us since birth. We can begin to remove all the beliefs we adopted over the years that aided our pursuit of enjoyment but hindered our ability to authentically thrive. When we no longer limit our being, our genuine self, we can fully connect with life and with others. This is the way to live wholeheartedly—to truly live and be radically accepting of who we really are. Our goal should be to learn to accept ourselves and our reality fully, to look within with curiosity and actively search for what lights us the fuck up and emboldens our spirit.

Our authentic spirit can only be liberated if we remove the mask we've placed over it. Within each of us is a deep longing to show our authentic selves and be loved, accepted, and seen for who we really are. Out of fear, we adapt to meet the expectations of who we think we must be for others to like us. We sacrifice authenticity for acceptance. But that is only half-living. We feel fully, truly alive when we move beyond fear and expose our genuine selves.

"It is better to be hated for what you are than loved for what you are not."

ANDRE GIDE

Being hated blows ass, but the thing is, until you can accept who you really are and expose that part of yourself to the world, you are subconsciously flipping yourself the bird. If we limit our being, we sacrifice true self-love for superficial love from others. Until we learn to love and accept ourselves fully and completely, we cannot truly love others or be truly loved in return. To feel the absolute, deep, powerful love within each of us, we must first show that love toward ourselves. Doing so will connect us to authentic living and, as a result, authentic loving.

There is a magnetism to people who live authentically because their authenticity is something everyone craves but so few achieve. Being authentic can be scary as fuck, because it puts who we really are on the line and in a position to be judged. What if we learned to let go of that fear, and realize that when we are authentic and speak and act from our heart, it is an inspiring, primal wake up call to others to engage their true being? Let us lead by example and ignite a revolution of authenticity. It will trigger an awareness of our connectedness and commonalities as fellow human beings. We are all the same and yet we are all unique. Perhaps that shared uniqueness is the common thread.

Deep down in every human's core is a place of love. When

we can make decisions from that place, we can cultivate deep connections. It takes a shit-ton of courage to recognize the vulnerability and risk of presenting our full selves to others, and then do it anyway. When the voice in your head criticizes or judges you, thank it for trying to protect you and tell it you know what you are doing and it is A-Okay. That voice, destructive as it may be, is just trying to help you survive. It is trying to prevent you from feeling shame or rejection. Ironically, when it kicks into overdrive it creates the exact emotions it is trying to prevent. Again, we are presented with an opportunity to learn the art of letting go. Graciously thank the mind and let it know that you are going to use your heart for this one. The mind will try to trick you into thinking this life is about separation and self. But when we connect with the heart, we tap into the awareness that we are, cliché as it sounds, all one. And for us to thrive as individuals, we must place our focus on what we can do to let *others* thrive.

Our purpose is to find what is authentic and true within ourselves and live that truth through love, growth, learning, and gratitude. When we are authentic, we can be open to serving others more fully. We can present the world with our unique gifts based on our individual experiences, and that is what service is all about. Expressing our gifts through our unique authenticity. By placing our focus on others, we can help ourselves. To live our best life, we must connect with our heart to express our genuine nature in a way that helps others.

All of life's experiences, particularly the challenging ones that invite our inner asshole to come out and play, are opportunities to learn through the application of our authenticity.

They are tests of character intended to make us better. The harder or more intense the experience, the more life is pushing us to grow beyond our current state and move forward while remaining true to who we are. If we can become grateful for each of these learning experiences and see them as life's intervention to get us onto the right path for us, we can let go and surrender with clarity. We can see that by trusting in the journey, through all its twists and turns, we will arrive at the most incredible destination. A destination that was made beautiful because of, not in spite of, the challenging experiences we faced along the way. The result will be just as remarkable as the paths we took to arrive there. It will be much easier along the way if we ease up off the brakes and just roll with it as authentically as we can.

JET LAG TOOL KIT
HOW TO CONNECT TO YOUR TRUE SELF

1. **Reflect on who you think you are as a person.**
   Ask yourself:
   - What do I believe in?
   - What are my values?
   - What do I like and love about myself?
   - What kind of person am I?
   - If I were to die tomorrow, how would I want to be described in my obituary?

2. **Be honest with yourself and really give this some thought: Are you currently living in alignment with the answers you just gave?** Reflect on how you act, speak, and think day to day. Is there a gap between who you think you are or want to be and how you behave? Examine the actions that shape that definition.

3. **What are the daily habits that contribute to making you who you are _at present?_** Be sure to look at the intentional and unintentional habits that influence your regular behaviors.

4. **Think of characteristics and values that constitute the absolute best version of yourself, the self you want to be.** Are they in line with what you answered above? **What can you regularly do to be true to the best version of yourself?** How do you need to think, act, and speak on an ongoing basis? What are the habits you need to change to support your ideal self?

5. **Repeatedly and consistently think, speak, and act in a way that your best self would think, speak, and act.** If your best self is patient, happy, and grateful, make an effort to think, speak, and act like a patient, happy, grateful person would.

CHAPTER SIX
OUTSIDE OF THE FIRE

ECUADOR

9:15am flight: T-2.5 hours

I pulled up to the Quito airport at 6:45am eager to begin my next trip. After three months of living in Ecuador I was going to meet my dad, stepmom, and stepbrother in Peru before heading to Bolivia for a one-week stay on the Amazon River. The timing would be tight, and a lot was riding on everything going well. My flight would arrive in Lima just a couple of hours before theirs. We would spend one night at the closest airport hotel before departing the following morning at the butt crack of dawn for Bolivia.

I got my boarding pass, checked my luggage, and was told to go through immigration prior to heading to the gate. I handed them my passport, boarding pass, and a printout of my return flight into Ecuador. After a brief review of the documents, the immigration officer gave me an annoyed look and asked, *"Y tu censo? ¿Dónde está tu censo?"*

Now, I had never heard of a *censo*, so the fact that they were asking for one thoroughly confused me and caused me to sweat profusely. After some frustration (on their part) and confusion (on my part), I learned that when I got to Ecuador, I was supposed to have registered for a *censo*, a sort of foreigner ID card, within thirty days. Something I definitely hadn't done. The officer said I couldn't leave the country without one. Seeing my look of panic, they gave me an address for a government office that could give me a temporary document, enabling me to board the plane and take care of the official *censo* upon my return.

"My flight boards at 9:15. Will I even get it in time?" I asked.

They shrugged and offered a *buena suerte* for good measure. *Good luck.* Considering that nothing moves quickly in Ecuador, I was definitely going to need it.

I ran out of the airport without any luggage, since I had already checked it, and hopped into the first cab I could find. Now, there is something to note here. At that time, Ecuador was dealing with a pesky issue of "Express Kidnappings," especially among cabbies. And especially in Quito. And especially at the airport. Basically, folks impersonating cab drivers would kidnap people and drive them around the city to every type of ATM, wiping out their funds. As a result, there were warnings and suggestions posted around the airport to always call a cab rather than hailing one. Unfortunately, I didn't have that kind of time. So, I hoped for the best and got in.

I explained my time-sensitive dilemma to the taxista and a look of pity and concern washed over his face.

"Espero que la oficina esté abierta," he said as he shook his head and sighed: "I hope the office is open."

He sped through the city, we arrived at the address, and I saw a line of about twenty people and a "Closed" sign on the door. The office wouldn't open for another fifteen to twenty minutes.

T-1.5 hours to flight. I paid the taxista and he kindly got out to ask the office guard what I would need to get the temporary *censo.* As expected, the guard responded with more bad news. I would need a color copy of my passport, visa, registration, and entry stamp, in a manila envelope. I had none of these things. The copy shop next door was closed.

The taxista said he would try to return after a couple more fares and wished me luck. I took my place in line, watching him walk away, filled with despair and with no idea how I would pull this off. I felt any remaining hope that I would make my flight and see my family disappear. Worry consumed my thoughts. Blame followed shortly after. I was so pissed at myself for not knowing I needed to register, and I felt my mood plummet. I felt defeated. Numb and angry. Then, I looked up to see the taxista running towards me. After getting into his taxi, he had changed his mind and decided to come back to help me, a complete stranger.

"¡Vámanos!" he shouted.

We were going to find a copy shop and make sure I made my flight. We ran for four blocks until we found one that was open, got the copies, ran back, and still had a couple of minutes until the office opened. By this time, there were about forty people standing in line.

The taxista begged the guard to let me in now and go first, and he must have said the magic words because it worked. Within ten minutes I received a temporary *censo* valid for thirty days, which was absolute record time for accomplishing anything in an Ecuadorian government office (think DMV x 100). We were on the road again, weaving through mid-morning traffic, dodging street dogs, both of us yelling at pedestrians to move it or lose it. I got to the airport with thirty minutes to spare.

I wasn't sure if Ecuadorians even used the phrase, but I told the taxista he was a lifesaver. He humbly shook off my attempt at explaining how genuinely grateful I was for his help and how indebted I was to his generosity. I handed him triple the amount his meter showed for the fare, and he tried to turn it down, but I insisted. It just goes to show that there are still good-hearted people in the world willing to go completely out of their way help a total stranger. I said goodbye and for the third time that morning was told "Good luck." I had already received more than my share that morning.

Once again, I was running through the airport like the cast of *Home Alone*. I reached my gate just as they did the final boarding call. I'd made it. *Gracias al taxista.*

People react to scarcity in different ways. Some people shut down while others rise up. Some focus on blame, anger, victimization, and self-importance, while others commit to compassion, determination, and positivity. Life will occasionally throw you crazy-ass curveballs, and that day taught me that in those moments of unforeseen chaos we must resist the temptation to be consumed by what is lacking, which guarantees a self-centered focus and causes us to act in contradiction to our values. That taxista reminded me to lean into the moment and accept it as though it was given to me. When we focus on others, we see with clarity and uplift the present situation, transforming it into a moment of grace and an opportunity to practice living in line with our values.

FEAR'S ALTER EGO

If you peel back the layers, you can see that a perception of scarcity is always rooted in fear of there not being enough (time, money, food, fill-in-the-blank). People are rarely the best versions of themselves when they're scared shitless. When scarcity is present, people revert to competitiveness and a self-centered focus to get their needs met. People feel their actions are justified or that once they secure what is scarce, they will be able to be their best self. But what if each moment of scarcity is a test to see if we truly embody our values?

What I propose is that we view moments of scarcity with a different mindset, seeing it as an opportunity to practice living in alignment with our values. For the present moment to happen, an infinite number of moments, choices, acts of will, and synchronicities had to take place. If you feel like there is not enough time, then that's all the more reason for you to pause, look around, and acknowledge the gift of that moment. Every moment that passes exists for you to uplift and participate in. Any moment in which you decide that instead of rushing to get to where you need to go you will be aware of whatever life is presenting you with and choose to participate in reality is a moment of grace. You'd be surprised how moments like this can guide you on a path that would have otherwise been invisible to your rushed eyes.

The more you develop a mindset of abundance, the more you see the countless magical moments that constitute your daily life. Some of us are so firm in our plans that we are completely blind to the situations that will catapult us into growth.

Scarcity is based on fear of not being or having enough. In times of scarcity, recognize that you still have the option to choose love over fear. Choosing love will be your compass, guiding you toward a life of grace, joy, and kindness. The root of almost all emotional reactions is deep-seated fear or pain. Anger, resentment, frustration, worry, sadness, impatience, assholery: So many of our most common negative reactions come from fear buried so deep we hardly recognize it. Peel back each reaction layer by layer to see the root. Is your anger solely focused on the present moment, or is it based on past events that have created a bias in how you view situations like this one?

If you had a deep wound on your leg that refused to heal and someone was gross enough to lightly graze it with their fingertips, it would feel much more intense than if they touched your leg in a spot that wasn't injured. The emotional scarring you build up over the years creates a bias in your reactionary states, often resulting in an over-the-top shitfit in response to a situation that would breeze by someone who didn't have the same emotional injury. When something kickstarts a negative response, take a breath and ask yourself if your reaction is based on some unresolved past fear or pain that's making you view the present with bias. To find peace, your goal is to let go of all that emotional baggage that has turned your psyche into a super-sensitive drama llama that overreacts to anything that touches it.

Easier said than done though, right? One of the best ways to let go is through witness consciousness. When a negative emotion comes up or some old bullshit is triggered, we typically allow that emotion to consume us. We can't think clearly because we are so focused on the thing that is upsetting us. It kicks up all the past shit related to the current situation, stacking examples of previous hurts and building up a self-righteous list of justifications for your reaction. Let that bull-honky go. Witness your reaction. You can separate yourself from your emotion by labeling what you are feeling. The words you use are important in this exercise. Rather than thinking, *Man, I am angry!!* think, *Hot damn, I* feel *anger right now.* To *feel* an emotion rather than *be* an emotion is an important shift. Words have power. They can subconsciously nut-punch you or give you a mental high-five. When you actively choose the words you use, your subconscious follows suit.

So, when something pisses you off or bums you out, pause and identify the emotion you are feeling. Do so with curiosity and self-compassion. Observe with interest and acceptance. No need to try to change it, that will happen automatically when you become aware of how that emotion affects you. After identifying it and noticing your physical response, try to dig deep to see why you are so upset by the situation. Be honest with yourself. Is it based on some past situations that were similar? Is it somehow based on a deep-seated fear or pain? Fear of not being seen or understood? By taking a brief pause to honestly reflect on what you are feeling and accurately identify it, you'll create detachment between yourself and the emotion, which allows its intensity to dissipate.

"A moment of patience in a moment of anger prevents a thousand moments of regret."

ALI IBN ABI TALIB

There are so many moments in life that cause us to freak out and have a grown-up temper tantrum. During those moments, we are given the opportunity to practice living in alignment with our values and responding to a situation like a well-functioning grown-ass adult. Regardless of how much you work on yourself, there will always be something that rattles you and makes you lose your shit. Life will keep ramping up the situation's intensity trying to get you to develop a broadened perspective and greater clarity, like how an athlete increases the weight they lift as they grow accustomed to larger and larger dumbbells. That is how to keep growing and get stronger. You need those opportunities to happen so you can practice with real-life experiences. It is much easier to stay calm and grateful in an enjoyable state. The true practice comes during moments of challenge.

These moments of practice could be as ordinary as getting stuck behind a super slow driver who's camping out in the fast lane, oblivious to the speed limit. Sure, that person could be an idiot who sucks at driving. But maybe they just found out that a loved one passed away and they're deep in thought. Or maybe they recently got in a horrible accident and are letting fear control the gas pedal. The reason doesn't matter. It's your response that does. Remember, the only two things you can control in life are your attitude and your effort. That's it. So, in the situation mentioned above, you might initially react with rage (especially if you are running late), but if you are able to rein that rage in and switch it to compassion through what-ifs (what if they just got terrible news?), it will give you perspective. By pausing briefly, you create space to detach yourself from your reaction just enough so it doesn't consume you.

It is not a bad thing to feel anger, frustration, or resentment. These negative emotional states are natural for all human beings. The key to preventing them from becoming damaging is how often and how long you entertain them. Consistent anger, frustration, or resentment can be detrimental to living your best life. They can embitter you, placing a salty veil of negativity over everything in your life. It's time to lift the veil. Ironically, to lift it, you must first let yourself feel it fully.

The Guest House

This being human is a guest house.
Every morning a new arrival.

A joy, a depression, a meanness,
some momentary awareness comes
As an unexpected visitor.

Welcome and entertain them all!
Even if they're a crowd of sorrows,
who violently sweep your house
empty of its furniture,
still treat each guest honorably.

He may be clearing you out
for some new delight.

The dark thought, the shame, the malice,
meet them at the door laughing
and invite them in.

Be grateful for whoever comes,
because each has been sent
as a guide from beyond.

— Rumi, translated by Coleman Barks

The more you try to stifle an emotion, the stronger it gets. You might try to stuff it down and distract yourself from it, but that just keeps it buried deep inside of you, growing stronger until the next situation that ignites that same response. Chances are, because that emotion is stacked from previous events, your reaction will be amplified and exaggerated, causing you to completely lose your shit. Then, you'll feel like crap, and you'll stifle those emotions until the next time, creating an impossible-to-win loop of losing your shit, feeling like crap, and stuffing down, growing in intensity with every anger-inducing event.

The alternative to stifling these emotions can be just as damaging. Hanging onto anger, frustration, or resentment builds up its intensity and power. Think of how many shower arguments you've reenacted (and won). Yeah, it feels good to give Susan the perfect comeback to her bitchy comment with shampoo suds covering your locks. But that *hell-yeah-fuck-you* feeling is short-lived, because it is masked in self-righteous anger. Every time you replay the moment in which you were wronged, it gives the negative emotion more strength, grows the anger, and adds bitterness, which turns into resentment.

"Resentment is like drinking poison and then hoping it will kill your enemies."

NELSON MANDELA

Chances are your replaying and reliving of the moment is disproportionate to the moment itself. And yet you continue to dwell on it for hours, days, weeks, sometimes years. What a waste! Talk about giving the other person power and letting them win. What they did may only have lasted a few minutes and yet you bear the destructive residue years after the fact. That is on you, not them. You cannot blame the other person for how long you choose to hold onto the anger.

Let's say you have $86,400 in your bank account and someone steals $10 from you. Would you let your anger compel you to spend $500 to get the $10 back? Or maybe you're willing to spend $5,000? What about $86,390? Would that be worth it? Fuck no! Well, we have 86,400 seconds in every day—so why on earth would you let someone's negative ten seconds ruin your other 86,390?

How do you avoid stifling or replaying anger, frustration, and resentment? The key is to learn to feel it, then let it go. This is obviously much easier said than done, but with practice it does get easier. One of the best ways to release the grip of a negative and all-encompassing emotion is to examine what it does to you physically.

Let's say you get home from a long, exhausting day at work, one in which nothing went your way. You open the front door to find your house looking like a turd tornado just blew through it. Your spouse forgot to take the trash out even though they said they would. Dirty socks are scattered on the floor. Food-crusted dishes are in the sink. You feel like you are not being seen or appreciated. Anger starts to build exponentially. At this exact moment, take a big ass breath. Then observe with a sense of curiosity the physical sensations of your anger. You may notice that you've clenched your fists and jaw, your stomach has tightened, and your breathing has gotten shallower. A small facial butt crack has formed between your eyebrows and your feel heat flushing through your body. Notice it. Observe it. Identify it. Acknowledge it. Think, *So this is what anger feels like. Okay, interesting. Thank you, anger, I choose to let you go now.* Then unclench and relax your body with a couple of deep breaths, while being aware of the physical change of release.

Stuffing it down will only cause it to become stronger the next time it occurs. To let go of an emotion you must experience it, not embody it. *Embodying* a feeling causes you to get lost within the emotion instead of letting it pass through you. *Experiencing* it enables you to learn from it and then let it go. The distinction between embodying and experiencing an emotion may be confusing at first. It can help to think of the emotion as a fire. If you are embodying the emotion, you are within the flames, feeling the heat, getting burned like a human s'more. You have no perspective on what lies outside it. All you can focus on is the heat and intensity. Experiencing the emotion, however, is like sitting next to the fire. You feel the heat, but you do not let it consume you. Because you have a degree of separation, you have greater understanding of the situation and can clearly react and respond.

Just the act of identifying an emotion and experiencing its physical response can pull you from the heart of the flames and make the heat bearable. You may even begin to appreciate and see the value in its warmth. Each time you do this, you're flexing the ability to choose awareness and perspective over anger—and refusing to let that anger hijack your emotions.

LISTEN TO LEARN

"The world is changed by your example, not by your opinion."

PAULO COELHO

In recent decades, a shift has occurred within our culture. The advent of social media has transformed the way we interact. We attempt to satisfy our need for connection by going online, which is just a temporary fix for the longing we feel to engage with others. You see, we were born with a deeply ingrained need to belong, to be a part of a group or tribe. Back in the day, this was a means for survival. To be part of a group or community meant protection from outside forces. Now, few of us face the same threats we once did, yet that need to belong still exists. Connection with others keeps us happy and healthy. The problem is that we've come to seek that connection via social media, which is analogous to trying to get lucky by watching porn. It is a cheap fix that may satisfy us on the surface but does not remedy the deeper need.

Social media is an arena where people choose how their virtual self is portrayed, often leaving out the vulnerability that fosters the trust and belonging necessary for genuine connection. People surround themselves with those who have similar opinions and views, and it results in a harsh, mob-like tribe that views differing opinions as a personal attack. This sort of interaction promotes an air of hostility and intolerance, leading to harsh and extreme behavior online. People use the masks of their virtual personalities to say things they would never dream of saying in a face-to-face interaction. It is a false conviction of righteousness backed by a mob-mentality of superficial tribalism.

By surrounding ourselves only with people who share our opinions, we reinforce our beliefs and close off the space needed for open-minded dialogue. But by having discussions inspired by curiosity with folks with differing belief systems, we are able to learn and grow. Let's seek the humility necessary for growth and remember that if we lived the exact same life with the exact same experiences as the person we disagree with, chances are we would share their same opinion. Each of us has had a lifetime of experiences that have shaped who we are and what we believe. Let's use our differences of opinion as an opportunity to learn how to respect and appreciate the varying beliefs of others. It is time to see our differences as potential strengths. We can counterbalance the intolerance of our hostile disagreements by applying compassion and open-mindedness to our conversations. If we do, we might actually learn something. We might begin to grow. We might begin to see that we are much more alike than we are willing to admit.

We tend to tie ourselves to our beliefs and ideas and defend them with fierce rigidity when they are questioned. If a person doubts our point of view, we feel compelled to defend it as though our honor is being attacked. An attack on our correctness is an attack on our pride. Have you ever had a disagreement about who was right? You believed one thing and they believed the opposite, but each of you were sure you were right? Then, after some more discussion, you likely realized that, oh shit, maybe there was a chance you were wrong? If you're like most people, you probably continued to defend your point despite no longer believing you were one hundred percent right. No way could you admit defeat after such a heated defense, because now your ego was involved. To admit you were wrong to a person who was so adamant they were right would somehow lessen you, because your pride is on the line.

When ego and pride are involved, we're more strongly tied to the idea we defend, regardless of whether it's correct. This involves a dance of grace between the two folks in discussion. The person who is incorrect must nut up and let it go. Admit that you may have been mistaken. The person who is correct also needs to nut up and be kind. "That's an interesting view that I hadn't considered" is a phrase that can save both your friendship and your ego. Often, if you continue to insist you're right to prove someone else wrong, you prove nothing but the fact that you are a pompous anal bead. Instead, both parties should seek to understand the other's point of view, listening to learn rather than to agree or disagree. Untie the connection between being right and preserving your pride, and you'll create space for constructive dialogue instead of closed-off arguments.

So many of the interactions we have result in frustration because we feel like we were not being heard or acknowledged. Here's the trick, though: You will not be heard by someone until you are able to hear them and make them feel understood. You must first listen if you wish to be heard. If you're getting riled up because of a disagreement, stop and ask yourself if you think the other person feels heard and seen. Focus on hearing them and listen with compassion and curiosity. Once you fully let them speak their truth and ensure that they feel heard, you will likely be given the space to speak your truth. Sometimes, though, the other person still won't hear your point, even if you've listened to theirs. In that situation, you just have to try your absolute best to calmly articulate your side and then let it go. Let it go through witness consciousness and compassion. Recognize that if they can't hear you right now that's fine, and keep on doing your thing.

Be careful not to fall into the trap of judgement. When we don't feel heard, it's easy to judge the other person harshly and create a mental story about how much of a dickwit they are. This quickly spirals into an out-of-control blame game based on self-righteous anger, which can snowball into thoughts like, *Humanity is really going to shit. This is the reason there is so much destruction and violence in the world. People like them are ruining everything. It's all their fault.* Stop blaming others. Instead, be the change you want to see. Lead by example. If you take responsibility for your words and actions, you will create a ripple effect of good intention.

It's up to you to live with integrity and embody the values and behaviors you expect of others. Seeking to prove that someone is wrong only hinders your growth and wastes your time. Focus on how you can serve or help others, which may come in the form of listening with genuine interest and curiosity. You have the power to make a positive impact, and that power begins with respect and love for all mankind, regardless of their beliefs. In all of your disagreements, search for the similarities that unite us, wear a compassionate heart on your sleeve, and keep an open-minded inquisitiveness and a desire to learn.

JET LAG TOOL KIT
HOW TO GET OUT OF THE FIRE SO YOU CAN ENJOY THE HEAT

1. **Check in with your body.** When a situation occurs that brings on an angry (or frustrated, or resentful) response, notice the physical change that occurs. Look at it with a sense of curious observation.
2. **Breathe.** Big, full, deep-ass breaths. Slowly exhale.
3. **Hang onto gratitude.** Say to yourself, "Thank you, anger/frustration/resentment, but I choose to let you go now."
4. **Watch yourself relax.** Feel the physical sensations of anger relax and release as you breathe.
5. **Shut down the endless loop.** If you replay or relive the anger, repeat this process, and ask yourself how many of your 86,400 seconds you are willing to waste on that moment.

CHAPTER SEVEN
THE GIFT YOU GIVE YOURSELF

FREEDOM THROUGH FORGIVENESS

When we hold onto the wrong that's been done to us, we give it strength far beyond its original power. Holding onto hurtful moments and grudges embitters us, eating away at our ability to experience joy. The only solution is to forgive. Consider forgiveness a gift you give yourself, not to the one who has wronged you. Forgiving someone enables you to remove the great burden of hurt from your shoulders so you can let that shit go once and for all. Until you learn to forgive—both others and yourself—you can't be at peace.

A common misunderstanding is that forgiveness means condoning the actions of the wrongdoer—which some might see as a sign of weakness. But the opposite is true. It takes a crapload of courage to forgive someone who screwed you over, and it's a true expression of love and acceptance. To forgive is to acknowledge what's been done to you with compassion, then choose to let it go, recognizing that everyone is doing the best they can.

Forgiveness is not about forgetting. It's looking at a situation with empathy, grace, and a larger perspective. It's reminding yourself that life is always happening *for* you, not *to* you. The most painful situations are those in which you're asked to learn the most. Use them as a reminder of what you're being asked to learn. How can you grow? How can you practice what you've learned so far in life? How can you try to see the situation from the wrongdoer's point of view? Can you attempt to view the event with compassion?

A compassionate approach enables you to kickstart the

letting-go process. Horrible shit happens to people, things that are completely unfair and undeserved. Sometimes, though, we unknowingly contribute to the event and are partially responsible for it. In both circumstances, if you apply compassion to your response and actions, you will be able to move on without hardening your heart.

The other person wins if you become embittered. It takes the event from a brief moment to one that entangles itself like a web of negativity over your relationships—including your relationship to yourself. It keeps you from living fully and developing the meaningful connections that bring value to life. When we close off our hearts, we eliminate the opportunity for healing connection.

Some people try to resolve the hurt by cutting the offender out of their life. They ice them out, building a wall so high and strong it will never be penetrated by that person (or anyone else) again. The problem is that the walls we build around our hearts don't protect us—they imprison us. Cutting someone off can certainly provide relief from the strife they've caused, but it doesn't remove the hurt at the root. It is just a matter of time before another situation pokes at that same wound. Closing off and shutting down creates a callousness that, if not resolved, will turn into bitter resentment. It's not the answer for those who truly want to heal. Once again, the more we try to avoid the pain, the more power it will have over us.

The healing, sustainable, yet far more difficult solution is to maintain an open heart through the process of forgiving, letting go, and moving on. The goal should not be to expel all hurt by shutting everything out. The goal should be to choose resilience, compassion, and growth to liberate yourself completely. This absolutely does not mean you should let someone repeatedly dump their shit all over you. It's about letting someone go and moving on, rather than cutting them out and closing off your heart. One is based in love (for yourself and others), the other in fear (of getting hurt again). Always choose love.

To do this, you need to find value in the suffering you experienced and attempt to see how each and every moment is happening for you. The wrong that took place is the reality. It happened. No amount of resistance or judgement will change that. So, the first step is to accept it. You realize that what happened, happened. It's done. Then, ask yourself, *If life is always happening for me, what lesson or gift is this situation trying to show me?* Maybe it's an opportunity for you to practice forgiveness or compassion. Or a chance for you to apply perspective and see what part you may have played in what occurred. There is *always* a lesson or a gift. You just have to search for it. It may not show up right away, and that is A-Okay. But it will. Trust that. If you look for it, you will find it.

The more a situation upsets or unsettles you, the more you are meant to pay attention. It is life trying to shake you awake. Change your attitude and you change your life. If you look at the pain and hurt you feel as a gift or opportunity, your whole world changes. Typically, as we learn and grow, we find a theme or pattern to the disturbances that repeatedly plague us, amplifying in intensity as we move through life. Life is all about progress. As long as we are growing and improving, we're living. Progress is an innate part of who we are, and one of the key components to happiness. So, if we overcome one pain-inducing event, the next to occur may be even stronger. It's our slightly ass-backwards way of developing emotional resilience.

Forgiveness provides you with freedom from your mind's reactions. Forgiving yourself or others is the first critical step on the pathway to inner peace. The second step—just as important, yet often overlooked—is to let go of the part of you that felt wronged in the first place. What is the source of the pain you've held onto, the one so disturbed by what happened that you felt forgiveness was necessary? If we can let go of the piece of us clinging to what happened, then we can survive anything life throws our way. If we can adopt the belief that life is always happening for our personal growth, we will begin to view circumstances in a much healthier and more empowering way.

Some say that you can't fully forgive another until you learn to forgive yourself. To truly be able to express compassion or love, you must first be compassionate and loving toward yourself. I know this sounds a little woo-woo, but it can be easier to grasp if we imagine forgiving the kid version of ourselves. Let go of thinking about how weird or stupid this is and just try it out. Begin by closing your eyes and picturing yourself as a kiddo. Visualize what you looked like, how your voice sounded, and how you were dressed. Think of the thing you did that you still can't forgive yourself for—not necessarily as a child, but at any time in your life. Accept what happened as reality. You cannot change it. All you can change now is your view of it. For suffering to have value, you must give it meaning. Let go of whatever you have been holding onto and feel compassion for the child-you. Forgive them (think or say "I forgive you"). Trust that what happened was part of your journey and reflect on what you learned from it. Grow from it. Then let it go.

The grudges we hold onto bring us down and keep us from living up to our full potential. They taint the way we view situations and create a subconscious bias for all that we see and do. These grudges are typically formed without us realizing it. Past hurts stack on top of one another, creating a seemingly impenetrable callus on the psyche. To have any hope of viewing a situation with clarity and grace, we must heal the scars that have formed. By patiently and compassionately reflecting on the grudges we have been carrying, then detaching ourselves from them, we can acknowledge them for what they are: opportunities to cultivate gratitude. Each was a lesson. Each was a gift. Each was a chance to practice letting go.

The best solution is always the one based on love over fear, being open over closed, and finding connection rather than separation. Reflect on your part in the situation that hurt you, focusing on the lesson hidden in that hurt. Attempt to forgive by repeating "I forgive you" every time you think of the wrongdoer. With time, the pain will fade. You will be able to learn and grow. You will begin to heal.

The more difficult it is to look at an event that hurt you, the more inner work you are doing. If it's hard as hell, that's a good sign! It means you are shifting things inside yourself, moving long-stagnant emotions around, and doing a bit of spring cleaning for your soul. Dust will arise and cloud your intention, and that's a good thing. You're shaking the shit out of your emotional snow globe. Continue to bring up the pain points and focus on breathing through them, giving thanks for what they taught you, then releasing them. Keep doing this repeatedly for as long as it takes for everything to settle. Eventually, it won't hurt as much when you think of these emotional injuries. With time, you'll feel genuine gratitude for the pain. You'll recognize that it provided you with a needed lesson, and the gift will uncover itself. Trust this process.

JET LAG TOOL KIT
HOW TO FREE YOURSELF
FROM PAST GRUDGES

1. **Think of a time when you were wronged by someone.** Perhaps as you do, you start to tense up and your panties get all twisted. Observe the physical response to the thought of that person and event with curiosity. Then try to focus your attention on changing your breathing so it grows deep and slow. As you replay the event in your mind, put yourself in the wrongdoer's shoes. What type of life would they have had to live to behave the way they did? If you were given their exact same life, might you have done the same?

2. **Focus on cultivating compassion towards that person.** Ask yourself if anything you did might have contributed to their actions. Could you have communicated more clearly? Continue breathing deeply, and repeat, "I forgive you." Remind yourself that forgiveness is a gift you give yourself, allowing you to liberate yourself from the event and

find peace. To forgive is to let go of the control someone has over you. Any time you think of the situation and feel prickles of hate or anger, repeat "I forgive you" continuously. With time, doing this will soften the part of you that was hurt, and the words will become true.

3. **Write it down.** Another helpful tool for forgiveness is one my grandmother taught me. If she was hurt by someone, she wrote a letter bitching them out. Man, she let them have it. All the anger she felt would fall onto that page. Once she was done, she would place it in her drawer, and—pay attention now—NOT send it. Occasionally, she would pick up the letter and read it, and if it still ignited anger, she would place it back in the drawer. Eventually the anger would subside, and the letter would no longer hold any power. Then she would destroy the letter.

4. **Look for the lesson.** At first, it might be difficult
   to find the good in a situation that resulted in hurt,
   pain, or anger, but you have to trust that it's there.
   One awesome tool for forgiveness is to look for
   the good that came out of the painful event. If
   you're feeling it, you might even think *Thank you*
   to the wrongdoer for doing something that, however surprisingly, led to something great

CHAPTER EIGHT
FINDING THE FUNNY

LIGHTHEARTED LIVING

Not taking ourselves—or life—too seriously is one of the most beneficial habits we can adopt as we make our way through this world. A sense of humor can transform a difficult situation into a manageable (or, dare I say, enjoyable) one. Over the course of human history, as life became more comfortable and less about survival, we started to amplify the seriousness of problems, turning minor upsets into disasters. Or, more elegantly put, we started making shitstorms out of dingleberries. As human beings, it is a part of our nature to search for threats or potential problems and do what we can to mitigate them. Originally, this was purely a survival technique, but since life is now so much safer and easier for much of the developed world, we revert to our ingrained response regardless of the seriousness of the situation. We create problems out of nothing.

We've all heard that the difference between tragedy and comedy is time. Once the sting of shock or disappointment begins to fade, we can view the situation with a more lighthearted perspective. What if we speed up the amount of time needed for us to transform a tragedy into something we can laugh about? What if we adopted a new outlook focused on finding the humor instead of the problem? No joke: If you search for the humor, you will find it.

Let's commit to lightening up! Laugh at yourself for how silly your seriousness has been. We all need a good dose of playfulness. Right now, as you read this, laugh out loud. Do it. Ha ha ha (there, I did it with you). Hopefully you aren't in public right now, or you're going to look pretty damn silly, huh? Even in the privacy of your own home, I bet that felt awkward as fuck. But guess what? The world didn't end. Let go of your self-judgements, relax, and lighten up. If you're quick to laugh, you'll be slow to anger.

Overcoming the auto-responses of shame, embarrassment, frustration, or anger through humor can defuse a situation that might otherwise haunt us long after its ideal expiration date. Stop ruminating over what went wrong and focus on the funny. Laugh more freely. Take a deep breath and smile. It's not that bad. The person who laughs first, wins. It's time to relax, let go of all the seriousness, and realize that with a lighthearted, playful attitude, even the shittiest of problems take on a lighter air and stink less. Laugh at yourself. Laugh at life. It is okay to make a mistake. Learn from it and let it go. If anything, you'll get a funny story out of it.

FOOD FOR THOUGHT

For a couple of months in my twenties I rented an apartment in Buenos Aires, Argentina. I spent my time wandering the cobblestone streets while looking for love in all the delicious places. I had many lovers, all edible in nature. There were the *alfajores*, two soft little cookies joined by a healthy dollop of *dulce de leche*, a rich, sweet caramel made from condensed milk. Depending on the brand, they would either be dipped in white or dark chocolate, or just left to be enjoyed in all their naked, undipped glory. Whoa mama, could I put those suckers down. I made it my mission to try as many types as I could find.

There was also *choripan*, a cleverly named chorizo sausage served on *pan* (bread), typically served by *choripan* carts that lined parks or busy sidewalks. Each cart provided a variety of toppings. My go-tos were grilled onions, spicy peppers, chimichurri, tomatoes, and hot sauce. Perfect-pan.

Now let's not forget what Argentina is known for! The glorious steak and wine. Goes together like…steak and wine. Just thinking about it makes me drool like Homer Simpson. In California, the cost of a good steak and bottle of wine at a restaurant can make you question whether you'll be able to afford groceries the following week. In Argentina, a full bottle of wine was the cost of just a glass anywhere else. Steak typically came with a simple yet profoundly flavorful chimichurri. It was the perfect marriage of food and I was the other woman, sampling both to my delight.

The nightlife in Buenos Aires was unlike anything I had ever experienced. For a twenty-six-year-old granny like me, it was hard to stay awake until the typical dinnertime of 10:30pm. I decided to fully own my geriatric gastronomy, going to nearly empty restaurants with a local newspaper in tow, attempting to read articles while highlighting words or phrases I didn't know (most wound up being very colorful). I learned that a typical Friday or Saturday night out involved a late and languid dinner (starting at 10pm at the earliest), followed by bars until around 2:30 or 3:00am, when the clubs and *discotecas* finally started to fill. Folks would dance until about 6am, after which came the afterparty; that went until about 9am. Woof. I could not keep up. I attempted a night like this one time, and *my* afterparty involved closed blinds and a comfy mattress.

More commonly I found myself in bed trying to sleep at around 11:00pm, only to hear young kids and families laughing on their way to a nice family dinner. *Keep it down, ya hear?!* I'd think, shaking my fist at the window. Granny Kathryn, indeed.

When you are new to a city and don't know a soul, you have a lot of time for reflection and observation. You notice a lot. The way people interact, the dynamics of a culture. Subtle differences that add an air of foreign magic and mystery to the commonplace. The best way to hail a bus can vary greatly by nation. In the United States, you simply stand at the bus stop, counting on the unspoken agreement that the driver will stop. In France, you wait at the designated bus stop and raise your arm the way you might in a restaurant to say "Check, please." In Ecuador, to gain the attention of any public driver, whether of a bus or a taxi, you raise a straight arm toward the vehicle, point the palm of the hand down, and flap it up and down like you are fanning a person who just fainted. In Guatemala, an *ayudante* shouts from the open door of a repurposed American school bus, colorfully painted and souped-up, advertising where they are going and trying to persuade you to catch a ride rather than walk.

Learning the common practices of a culture is a humbling experience, as is learning a new language. To keep your ego from crumbling, you need a sense of who-gives-a-shit humor. There are many false friends in the Spanish language that should be used with caution or, at the very least, a self-deprecating smile. For example, *sopa* does not mean soap in Spanish, but rather, soup. I can still vividly recall the look of confusion on my Ecuadorian host grandmother's face when I asked her what type of *sopa* she uses for the washing machine.

Beyond the words that sound similar but mean something different, there are the different meanings a word may have depending on the country. The verb *coger* in Ecuador means to take or to catch, as in *voy a coger el bus* (I am going to catch the bus). Use that same phrase in Argentina and you'll get a bunch of surprised looks, some impressed, others disgusted, since in that country *coger* means to fuck. I learned that one the hard way. When I was working as a waitress in California, I learned that Spain's word for drinking straw can mean either penis or marijuana cigarette in Mexican Spanish after I asked one of the cooks if they wanted a penis/joint with their water.

When we don't take ourselves or life too seriously, we start to see the humor in almost any situation. Laughter keeps us present and appreciative of the moment at hand. It helps us heal. Most of all, though, it lets us enjoy the journey no matter where we are.

JET LAG TOOL KIT
HOW TO LET GO
THROUGH LAUGHTER

1. **Embrace your inner goofball.** Let your weird, embarrassing, silly self thrive and stop judging so harshly. Vow to no longer take yourself or life so seriously.

2. **If something upsets you, try to laugh at it.** Appreciate life's humor and impeccable timing. Speed up the amount of time it takes to go from tragedy to comedy by accepting what happened and then letting it go.

3. **Smile and laugh more freely.** You will start to loosen up. Even if this means faking it 'til you make it. Smile and laugh even if you don't feel like it, and you will start to feel like it.

4. **Play!** Not everything you do needs to have a purpose. Do something for the sheer enjoyment of it and you will notice that your productivity increases in other areas of life. Ironically, play fosters productivity.

5. **Remember, if you actively look for the humor in life, you will find it.**

CHAPTER NINE
INTO THE STORM

CALIFORNIA

The foghorns acted as my alarm. I opened my eyes and saw my breath as I exhaled. The faded blue tent fabric began to come to life as the early morning sun crept higher. I stretched my stiff neck and back, trying to loosen up after sleeping on the ground without a pillow. A new day, one of adventure and obligation, prompted me to leave the warmth of my sleeping bag and get ready for school. I put on my slightly stained No Fear t-shirt and cutoff jean shorts, laced up my red high tops, then brushed my hair out with my fingers before tying it back into a low ponytail. As good as it was going to get, I was ready.

I unzipped the tent and a cold, misty breeze made me shiver. Nobody else was awake, so I gathered some wood and kindling to make a fire. Quickly enough, the crackling of burning wood filled my ears and added some percussion to the waves of the nearby ocean. I got as close to the fire as I could to capture its heat without feeling the burn—a practice I spent many mornings perfecting.

After about thirty minutes of solitude, I checked my *Lion King* watch and felt the stress of future lateness approaching. My school was a good forty-five minutes from the beach that had become our temporary home, and I absolutely hated being late. I already stood out enough, showing up every other week stinking of campfire smoke. As with most sixth graders, I just wanted to fit in. I tried making some noise in hopes of discreetly waking my mom and her boyfriend, Darren. Their tent remained silent.

My sister and Darren's three kids weren't scheduled to

stay with them this week, so instead of five, it was just me. I secretly enjoyed the extra attention but dreaded that getting to school on time landed solely on my shoulders. Seeing the clock ticking and feeling my overly responsible 12-year-old's anxiety begin to grow, I tossed a piece of driftwood at the tent hoping it would wake them. Nothing.

I nervously glanced at my watch again.

"Ahh, fuck it," I said under my breath, my sailor's mouth having developed at a young age. I shook the tent and with forced cheerfulness said, "Hey, time to go, sleepyheads!"

I heard the rustling of synthetic material while Darren and my mom emerged with keys in hand. I breathed a sigh of relief. Stomach growling, I grabbed my backpack, hopped in the car, and off we went, arriving just as the shrill final bell rang out across the schoolyard.

THE BEST OF BOTH WORLDS

My childhood was somewhat unique. I was like a pendulum, swinging back and forth between my mom and dad's very different lifestyles. To say they were opposites was an understatement. My mom has always been a very artistic and spiritual person, living a life based on following the heart and spirit. My dad was gifted with a natural ability in business, the perfect blend of intelligence and intuition. They divorced when I was three years old, and from that age until I was in high school, my sister and I had a classic child-of-divorce schedule: every other week we switched to the other parent's home. The homes varied over the years, and by the time I graduated high school I had moved homes nearly twenty times. One of my superpowers is the ability to quickly and effectively pack my shit in as few boxes as possible.

Most of the moves were my mom's. We went from apartments to houses to trailers to homeless and back to apartments. We typically moved because of financial reasons, or because of this or that bad boyfriend—and there was a succession of them over the years. My mom has always had a huge heart, choosing to see the best in everyone. Unfortunately, this attracted some not-so-great men, leading us to move around often as a way to "start fresh." After a breakup, one ex-boyfriend would come by late at night, pounding on the door trying to get in. Another would put Super Glue on our door locks and sugar in Mom's gas tank. But this was child's play compared to Darren, the most disruptive of them all. Their relationship uprooted our life and dropped it on its head.

Darren and my mom met when I was in fourth grade. I was best friends with his daughter, and they met on a sunny afternoon while picking us up from school. It was one of those encounters that radiated instant chemistry. They seemed to make each other feel alive, igniting something in each other that had been dormant. During the early months of their relationship, life was fun-filled and exciting. Darren didn't seem to care what people thought and lived life on his own terms.

Within a few months of when they began dating, we moved into his home, rumored to be an old crack house. Occasionally we had unexpected visitors who hadn't gotten word that a new family had moved in. When money got tight, we started moving: to deteriorating rat-infested houses and trailers, friends' couches, and finally, when I was twelve, a tent on the beach. As a preteen tomboy, I saw it as a big, slightly uncomfortable adventure. Reality is the meaning we give it, right?

Through all the moves, I became an expert at adapting to the unpredictable ways of a transient lifestyle, which fed a part of me that loved uncertainty and spontaneity. With five kids and no permanent place to stay, we rarely had a bed. Instead, we would unroll our sleeping bags and crash out on the floor of wherever we ended up.

Darren had an unconventional view on life, and in the beginning, it was refreshing. He felt that schooling should be based on a real-world curriculum and hard work. He owned a landscaping business and would often drop us kids at one of his job sites to use pickaxes, saws, and shovels unsupervised as he and my mom ran errands. For hours on end, Darren's three kids (my best friend at the time and her two younger brothers), and my sister and I would work on someone's yard, never knowing when our parents would return. Darren drove an old flatbed Chevy truck with one large bench seat, so when we went places, the five of us kids would lay in the truck bed under blankets to avoid being seen, sometimes for hours at a time on freeways to job sites or camping trips. We chased cheaper rent and half-baked, far-fetched opportunities that never delivered what my mom and Darren hoped they would. On to the next! It was an undeniable lesson in adaptation and resilience.

As the months passed, Darren's true colors began to show. He became physically abusive, manipulative, and cruel toward my mother. She developed breast cancer, and her longtime struggle with depression amplified severely, prompting suicidal behavior. There were times during their relationship when my mom went away for a while to what I later learned were either health facilities or safe houses, depending on the timing. Since I alternated every other week between my mother and father, much of Mom and Darren's relationship of codependent chaos and depression escaped my attention.

Eventually, the pain of staying outweighed the pain of leaving, and with new clarity and a broader sense of perspective, my mom began to plan. Change always comes about due to a tipping point. Eventually, pain prompts us to change. My mother got herself and my sister and I restraining orders against Darren and left.

On the completely other end of the spectrum was my dad's home. Dad was an entrepreneur who worked hard as hell to grow his business and offered his love through the act of providing. He worked hard and played hard, although during those early years the play was rare and limited. He did well for himself. We moved a couple of times over the years and typically lived in large homes on the outskirts of town, nestled on acreage with neighbors few and very far between. The homes would have large glass windows without blinds or drapes that overlooked the front and backyards, providing beautiful views during the day yet leaving you feeling exposed and vulnerable during the night.

Many nights my dad would attend a work event and my sister would go to a friend's house, leaving me home alone. The glass windows felt less fancy when it was pitch black outside, making me feel scared and unprotected. At nine, ten, even eleven years old I would hear something unsettling and feel like someone was watching me from outside. I would triple-check the door locks and hide under my bed until my dad got home several hours later, then finally fall asleep.

Since my sister spent most of her time at friends' houses or after school events, I often found myself alone for hours on end. I spent countless afternoons wandering the rolling green Northern California hills behind my dad's house with my dog, Sophie. I used my imagination to take me outside of myself and desperately tried to find magic within the common moments of life. I thought that if I believed hard enough, I would find it: some secret world that went unnoticed to the human eye, just below the surface of reality.

But over the years, my interests changed. My longing to be accepted and liked in adolescence took precedence over my imagination and the comfort I'd found within myself. Being alone transformed into loneliness, and it wasn't until years later that I relearned what I'd once known.

You can feel lonely when you are surrounded by other people and, conversely, feel accepted and loved when you are alone. As human beings, we crave connection. To experience love and connection, we must have love and connection within ourselves.

My upbringing gave me such an incredible view of the world. I lived in a beautiful, albeit often empty, upper-middle-class home one week and a rat-infested trailer the next. I saw such diverse lifestyles firsthand, and it gave me balance and perspective. I learned to be self-sufficient almost to a fault. Each of the experiences I had was purposeful and intended for my growth. They needed to happen for me to become the person I am now and will continue to become.

Many times, our moments of growth are hidden in moments of pain, sadness, or anger—life's way of giving you a loving little throat punch to grab your attention and push you to transform into the person you were meant to be. Leaning into the discomfort (pain, fear, anger) is what lets you improve. When you ignore it or try to force your way through it, life will continue to present the same situations until you feel them fully. The more you ignore the discomfort, the more prevalent it will be the next time.

What if the fateful moment of my fourth grade best friend and I walking to the parent pick-up area of our elementary school was life guiding me onto a path that would drastically alter who I became? What if instead of viewing all that followed as what some therapists have described as developmental trauma, I redefined it as some of the experiences that made me into the woman I have become? In retrospect, it's clear to me that both of my parents were doing the very best they could. The love they had for my sister and me was never lacking; it was just shown in unconventional ways.

Life gives us situations that put us on the path toward becoming who we are meant to be. Many times, those situations shake us to our core. Always, they provide us with an opportunity to learn or grow. The more challenging the situation, the bigger the insight will be.

What if you adopted a radically different outlook on the shitty experiences in your life? What if you learned to surrender and trust in all events you're presented with, recognizing them as reality? We often let our preferences cloud the truth of the present moment. If we can examine it for what it is—something that has already happened—and accept it as though it was chosen *for* us in order learn, grow, or express compassion and love, we can find genuine peace.

You get what you focus on. If you feel like you always get the shit end of the stick, you will subconsciously look for examples to support that opinion, further reinforcing that belief. Every experience we have had and the meaning we have given them create the story that shapes who we are. Two people can have the exact same event happen to them and yet each person can have a wildly different understanding of what occurred. Some choose to see the good and some choose to see only the bad. But how you view a situation doesn't change what happened. How you interpret reality is a decision, and it can either lift you up or bring you down.

Detach yourself from your opinions of reality and begin to view your life with a commitment to clarity. Choose to see life as a weaving together of moments that are happening for you exactly as they should, no matter how good or seemingly crappy. Choose to examine with earnest reflection the stories you have been telling yourself, and question whether they have been helping you grow or holding you back. What is the story you tell yourself? How have you been viewing the world? Is it through a perception of victimhood and self-pity, or growth and appreciation?

It's a choice. It doesn't matter whether you're eighteen or eighty, it's never too late to redefine your story. Now is the best time there is. Focusing on the good will shift your mindset so it starts to search for supporting examples of positivity. You will begin to see setbacks as opportunities, and notice that your reality is relative to your perception. Now is the time to choose an inspiring and uplifting view of your life.

The amazing thing is that we can always change our story. We can create a new meaning with every moment that passes. Daily life provides us with thousands of opportunities to practice viewing reality with clarity. As you move throughout your day, take a moment to pause and question if the meaning you are giving something takes away from the truth of what happened. Is the meaning based on past hurt and pain? Is it reinforcing a negative belief? Pause. Take a big-ass breath. Ask yourself if it could mean something different. How can you interpret a moment so it supports positivity and gratitude? How can you shift your perspective of a moment so you view it as something that is happening for your greatest good? Strip down and remove the biased layers of the past like a soul-seeking pole-dancer and see the present moment for what it really is. No excuses. No bullshit. Refuse to give in to the temptation to see yourself as a victim of circumstance. Don't let excuses keep you from achieving the happiness and peace of mind you deserve. Focus on committing to wholehearted authenticity, living your best life, and paving your pathway to greatness.

MOVING WITH THE STORM

Trusting in something we can't see is one of the greatest challenges we face. To have hope in times of despair is one of the bravest things we can do. We must lean into the vulnerability that consumes us when we are offered the opportunity to trust and surrender. Fear of disappointment can be debilitating, but to not try because of it is to not live fully. Life is filled with an infinite number of moments that call upon you to participate and step up. It's always your choice how you show up, if at all.

One of the greatest gifts we can give ourselves is to participate in each moment that passes before us and come at it with the fullness of our heart and soul. To attempt to bring our best selves forward in every opportunity and see, speak, think, and act out of love. When we look at the circumstances we face every day with eager anticipation and see the risk of disappointment, hurt, or pain yet choose to be open anyway, we free a part of ourselves that was never meant to be confined. It is that part within each of us that's receptive to the deep knowing that every single thing is happening as it should.

Think of the mighty redwood. This incredible tree is big as fuck. It can reach hundreds of feet high and live for thousands of years. When storms and high winds hit the redwood, it bends and moves with the wind, enabling it to outlast even the most severe weather. To resist and attempt to stand firm and unmoving would result in limbs and trunks snapping and breaking under the strain. The redwood has learned that to overcome even the harshest of attacks, its survival is dependent on easing up and going with the flow. Participating and dancing with the heavy winds and torrential rains lets it live.

The more we try to resist the tumultuous moments in life, the more quickly they will defeat and weaken us. There is a limit to how long we can resist the elements. In a state of rigidity, our energy is drained. But if we move with those moments instead of attempting to stand firmly, we find that flexibility allows us to maintain our energy and grow even stronger. By acknowledging the figurative (and literal) storms and high winds, we can bypass the first step of denial. We can see that it is happening and accept it. Through acceptance grows appreciation.

Lasting transformative growth tends to come from the greatest difficulties. It's in these challenging moments that our strengths are tested, and we are shaken into action and personal development. By learning to appreciate all of life's category-five turd tornados, we become able to recover more quickly from their devastating blows. And the meaning we give these events makes all the difference.

To attempt to fight or avoid the challenges only delays our growth and wears us down. To see it as done and unchangeable lets us choose our response rather than wallow in stagnant victimhood. When the storm begins to brew and the winds lash and whip, we first must acknowledge that the storm is a reality. A difficulty is happening. You lost your loved one. You got laid off from your job. You just got a diagnosis of terminal cancer. You are broke as a joke and just got evicted. You had a crappy childhood. Your opinion about how shitty it is does not change the fact that it happened. The storm has already arrived.

Now you have a choice. Do you resist it, or move and bend with the winds? If you choose to resist, be warned that it's just a matter of time before your energy drains from fighting and branches start to snap and break. Roots come up. Unnecessary chaos ensues. If you choose to move with the winds, you will reach peace more quickly. Sure, it'll be tough as hell, but it will be worth it. You know it will pass. You know that difficulties are a fact of life, and denying them will only keep you from their lessons even longer.

The storms shake loose seeds, and growth follows. With practice, you will accept the storms with quick clarity and move into a state of appreciation and trust. You will notice that each of the storms, as hard as they were, taught you how strong you are, and catapulted you into another phase of your life and purpose. Accepting them as part of your journey and appreciating them as you move through them with flexibility and grace will start to break down your flawed and detrimental conception of their perceived effects. Although the redwood's crown may sway fiercely in the wind, seemingly out of control, it is in fact a controlled, trusting dance grounded all the way down to the earth. It exists in harmony with the winds and grows stronger because of them.

My upbringing helped me grow stronger. The unpredictability of my mom's lifestyle shaped me and gave me the tools I needed for a resilient and adaptable lifestyle. The latchkey upbringing of my dad's lifestyle gave me the skills of self-sufficiency, independence, and imagination. I have needed every single one of the challenges I faced as a child to be prepared for my life as an adult. The skills I gained would not have been as ingrained in me if the challenges had not been as intense and demanding. As a kid, I just went with the flow, accepting what was going on because it was the only life I knew.

It wasn't until my late teens and twenties that I viewed the experiences I had as a kid as impediments and began to take on a view of rigidity and victimhood about my past. I felt like I was broken. The survival techniques I had adopted as a child began to harm me and hinder my growth because I was attempting to use them beyond their allotted time. I felt that to counterbalance the chaos and uncertainty of my childhood, I had to control everything in my adulthood. I swung from one extreme to the other. I had chosen resistance and rigidity in the face of life's storms, and in my desperate attempt to control, the winds nearly broke me.

It took me years to realize what I had known as a kid and then forgotten. The storms of my youth made me stronger. They happened because they were meant to happen, and my opinion of them did not change the fact that they occurred. I was in control of the meaning I gave my past, and of the meaning I gave my present. I decided I would not tolerate a meaning of victimhood and instead would choose empowerment. After years of trying to control everything around me in an effort to feel safe, I realized that the only thing I could actually control was the one thing I didn't think I had a choice over: the meaning I gave something. My attitude about a storm and my effort in enforcing a positive, grateful perspective is *always* my choice.

I learned that even though it took much longer than I'd like to admit, it's never too late to dance and move with the storms, no matter how long ago they took place or how little rhythm you have. The shit times are only damaging if you try to resist or blame them. Once you release the destructive meaning you give a challenge and replace it with one of empowerment and appreciation, you can begin to mend the past and pave the way for the future. You can begin to grow. You will realize that you can handle even the harshest of storms, and will welcome them with flexibility and grace, knowing that to dance in the howling winds is to thrive.

JET LAG TOOL KIT
HOW TO DANCE IN THE STORM
(EVEN IF YOU HAVE NO RHYTHM)

1. **Look back on your past.** Revisit some of the most difficult storms you've faced. Breathe deeply through the discomfort that comes up. Observe these past challenges with curiosity and without placing blame.

2. **Reflect on the gifts and growth these struggles have provided.** Find the value and benefit in the suffering. Search for the skills, lessons, and gifts you received.

3. **Accept the storm as reality.** Give thanks to it for what it taught you and appreciate that it led you to where you are right now.

4. **When new storms arise and the winds begin to howl, think of the redwood.** Choose to accept and appreciate the nature of the storm as a gift for you and your growth. Move with it, not against it. Remember that it will pass, and until it does, just try to enjoy the ride.

CHAPTER TEN
OWN YOUR SHIT

100% RESPONSIBILITY

There are two things you can control in life: your attitude and your effort. It doesn't matter where you are or what's happening, you always have the power to sack up and own that shit. Taking one hundred percent responsibility for your life comes down to choosing your reaction regardless of the fuckery that pops up throughout your day. It's the act of choosing the meaning you give a situation and the effort you make in response. When life takes a figurative dump on your chest do you think, *Why does bad stuff always happen to me? Now my day is ruined. Man, this stinks* (pun intended). Or do you think, *Ok, life, challenge accepted. I got this?*

Adopting an attitude of victimhood is debilitating to your personal growth. There are countless stories of people facing terrible atrocities and letting those moments define and limit them. Yet there are many others who have experienced equal or worse events who let those moments improve and uplift them. The difference is the choice they made: whether they view the situation as happening *to* them or *for* them. If you can adopt an empowering meaning for something that was difficult to withstand, you can overcome anything through grace and growth. It comes down to eliminating blame as an option and taking responsibility for your life.

Over the last several years, it seems that our culture has adopted a belief system focused on blame. People have gotten into the habit of vigilantly searching for a scapegoat in everyone and everything but themselves. They try to avoid personal responsibility at all costs. It's much easier to go through life placing blame on everyone else than it is to draw a line in the sand and say enough is enough, no more blame. Taking responsibility for your reaction is your duty. That's how you find the value in suffering and learn to thrive regardless of the circumstances. You choose to overlook the cheap and easy option of seeing everything that is wrong, noting all the problems, and adopting an attitude of victimhood. No good comes from this. No growth. No gratitude. It's time to create a dramatic shift in your views of the world and your life as a whole. It's time to take responsibility. It's time to take ownership over how you show up in the world.

We are given this gift of life without having to ask for it or work for it. We arrive in the world naked and slimy, heart beating, eyes open, with countless experiences awaiting us and our story patiently waiting to be written. We are born on different playing fields. Some win the jackpot and are born into opportunity, safety, education, and equality. Others are born into extreme poverty, danger, and corruption. By complete chance, some are given a huge head start just by where they were born. Let that shit humble you. If you're one of the lucky ones, born into the former, you must practice compassion and humility by appreciating the advantage you've been given. Regardless of where you were born and the resources and advantages you were given (or not) at birth, there is one gift that each one of us has and will always have. The power to choose. You have the power to choose your reaction to what life puts in front of you. It doesn't matter if you grew up in a one-room shack in rural Guatemala or in a five-bedroom house overlooking the California coast. The gift of choice does not discriminate. It's available to all of us and can be the key factor that levels the playing field.

Everybody's got problems. Granted, some folks may have better problems than others. But how we react to the challenges we face is up to us. The power of choosing our reaction can be described in many ways: changing our attitude, choosing how much effort we give, deciding whether we see life as happening to us or for us, etc. What it all comes down to is whether we take accountability for our life. To take one hundred percent responsibility for our life, our attitude, our effort, our reactions, our experiences, and heck, even our problems. It doesn't matter what you've experienced to this point. If you choose to take one hundred percent responsibility for your life, you will be forced to acknowledge that your attitude toward life is not dependent on external factors. It's generated within you. And hot damn, that's powerful.

We've all met people or heard stories of folks who have overcome incredible tragedy and hardship, having faced one extreme difficulty after another. And yet they have an unstoppable attitude and are unfazed by what life throws at them, regardless of how difficult it is. They don't let it bring them down and don't bother wasting their breath or thoughts on complaining. Victimhood does not serve them or give them their best life. By owning their shit and taking one hundred percent responsibility for their attitude and effort, they can handle anything that comes their way with grace, gratitude, and humor.

We've also all met the much more common type of person, who has had a pretty damn good life but finds the negative in everything. Sure, they have experienced difficulty, but overall, they have been born into a flourishing society and given a great advantage at birth and in life. This person focuses all their efforts on their problems and buys into the belief that they are a victim. They have a skill for seeking out what went wrong in any situation and are able to turn it into something that happened *to* them. What they don't realize is that they have everything within themselves to take a problem-filled life of victimhood and transform it into a life of fulfillment rooted in gratitude.

All it takes is a single choice. The decision to transform their expectations into appreciation and be accountable for their life. Only then can they see problems as gifts, opportunities given to them for their highest good and growth. Expectation generally leads to disappointment and comparison. If you swap expectation for appreciation, your outlook will drastically shift and force you to see the good. You'll realize that there is always something to be grateful for.

When you see that you always have control over your reaction, the appeal of the victimhood approach fades. So many of us use problems to feel important, destroying any chance of living a fulfilled life of genuine happiness. Sharing our problems for the sake of significance or victimhood provide us with a superficial, short-term gain of connection with others. People are sympathetic and caring...at first. But when a person becomes a chronic Problem Victim, friends and family start to grow tired of their incessant bitching. Usually this makes the Problem Victim attract more problems and an even worse attitude to get the response they crave. If this sounds familiar to you, stop that shit. It doesn't serve you long term. It weakens your relationships and ends up creating the opposite effect than the one you crave. People will eventually get sick of your constant complaints and negativity and try to avoid you.

I know this from experience. There have been times in my life when everything felt like it was going wrong. All I could focus on were the problems I kept getting hit with. I would reach out to friends and get caring responses of sympathy and encouragement. It made me feel better to have my negative attitude reinforced and feel the extra kindness from friends. But I found venting to be a slippery slope that quickly morphed into complaining. I noticed the sympathetic responses were no longer as sincere, because I had exhausted my friends as a resource. It took some humble soul searching but I began to realize that my negative view of reality was keeping me from seeing situations clearly.

Now, I'm not saying that you must abolish venting with friends entirely. If you are faced with a situation that kicks your "life is happening for me" attitude right in the ball sack, reaching out to a close friend or family member to talk it out can be very cathartic. Just be wary if it starts to become a habit. Venting can easily transform into complaining. And constant complaining can quickly turn you into a victim of circumstance. Just a reminder, nobody likes a Problem Victim. If you feel like you need to vent but have played the friend card one too many times, write out your feelings. Getting everything on paper can help clear your mind and give you some peace. Rage-write that shit out. Just don't give it to the person who caused you strife. That's just petty ass shit that only makes things worse. Writing it out produces words that are for your eyes only, and that method is a tool to be used to keep you sane and your friendships intact.

Recall a situation in your life that you have allowed to define you. A time when you placed blame instead of owning your reaction. Maybe it was a loved one dying, or getting abused at a young age, or getting laid off from a job you depended on. Blame does not necessarily mean just blaming another person. It can be the act of blaming anything, including the situation itself, for how it affected you or your life. Blame is the opposite of accountability. It's a weak choice, and when you blame, you become blind to the lesson. Blame is a waste of a moment. Instead, choose to take responsibility.

Responsibility is power. Responsibility is the act of adopting the deep-seated belief that everything that has ever happened in your life has happened for you and your highest good. It is the act of choosing to let that belief be your guiding compass, showing you what to take from a particular situation. Responsibility does not lessen the initial pain or hurt, but it does let you see the value and meaning in a given moment. It gives you the power of choice, which is one of the greatest strengths we have. Rather than trying to fight reality, those who take responsibility accept reality for what it is and then do everything possible to transform their reaction into one of empowerment and growth. They search for the value or the lesson. It exists in every moment, and it's our job to discover it. Trusting the process will assist us on our journey and allow us to lean on our firm belief that even though we may not see the good in the present moment, it does not mean there isn't one. It just means it hasn't fully unfolded yet.

Realizing that we have the option to shift our viewpoint can be unbelievably freeing. It can help us to let go of the bitterness of resentment that has developed over years of believing that the negativity we experienced served no purpose other than to make us suffer. Maybe there is a moment in your life that made you feel as though the only choice you had was to blame external factors. You let it harden your heart and close you off. Looking back on the reality of that situation, can you see that there was another option? Can you see any subsequent events that occurred because of that experience that led to something good? Honestly look at the chain of events that followed. What things happened in your life that would not have happened if not for that event? Search for the good. Perhaps it was something you learned. Or maybe it led you to meet someone new or gain some new insight. Maybe it was just the fact that you got back up again after the emotional Humpty Dumpty-esque fall.

What if every moment in your life, the good, the bad, and the painful, all happened exactly as they were meant to happen? What if each of those moments happened for you and your greatest good? If someone told you this, would you believe it? Sure, it's easy to have that mindset when things are going well and you are on a roll. But what about during moments of darkness? The most difficult moments in your life, the ones that you can barely stand to look back on for fear of drowning in shame or sadness or rage. What if even these moments were meant to happen, to guide you? How would your life change if you decided to look at it through a different lens—one that enabled you to see the greater picture and incorporate a deep trust in life and all that comes your way?

Think of your life as a painting. You go through life looking at the back of the canvas, not understanding the vision of the artist. Good and bad moments are represented with light and dark paint. Without seeing the finished product, you lament the dark paint, questioning why it must be used. But to create a masterpiece, there must be both light and dark paint. The contrast in colors creates depth and dynamism. We may not know why certain colors have been chosen yet, but once the painting is completed and the canvas is flipped, we can finally see and understand.

When life paints dark moments, let the light come from the value and meaning you give them. Choose to see the good. Recognize that you may not understand the artist's reasoning, and that's all good. What you must focus on is the *how*. How will you use that moment to better yourself or your life? It is always up to you. Don't wait until the end of your life, when the completed canvas is revealed to appreciate the beauty of the process. Take time throughout your life to look back on how the variety of colors have blended to create experiences that have guided you on your path. Reflect on life before it is over, and you will appreciate the journey before it is too late.

We need the bad times to become the best versions of ourselves. The adversities we face are what push us to grow and change the most. They are the moments that let us become stronger and put our potential to the test. Cliché as it is, there is some truth to "no pain, no gain." It is easy to apply all that we have learned about positivity and surrender during times where everything seems to be going our way. The real growth happens when we are faced with dark times and still put forth our daily practice of gratitude, surrender, and openheartedness. That is the challenge. But with consistent effort, it will become second nature. Even in times of great loss or pain, we will be able to have a bird's eye view of the event, expanding our interpretation of its meaning. By reminding ourselves that life's challenges are chances to practice looking for the benefit, the lesson, the gift, or the humor, we remove the feeling of helplessness and opt instead to act. When we search for the empowering meaning of a moment, we become empowered.

Don't get me wrong, there are so many moments when I forget this, falling back on my deeply ingrained habitual reactions of anger, frustration, hurt, or despair. Sometimes I get so caught up in my disappointment that something didn't go the way I wanted that I can't remember the whole "life's canvas looks better with some dark paint" thing. It can be really hard to remember to surrender in moments when that's the last thing you want to do. It is easy to fall back into the victim response of *shit just keeps happening to me*. When I react that way, it gives me temporary relief, allowing me to make excuses for why my life isn't going as I want it to: *It's not my fault. Look how hard I'm trying, and I just keep getting fucked (and not in a good way).* But excuses and blame are a short-lived fix, and will not serve me in the long run. So, I switch it up. I allow myself the brief pity party until I remember the wisdom I already know, then look for the benefit. I take responsibility where I can, even it's only in choosing my response. I try to be compassionate and patient with myself, no matter how long it takes, until I can change my view of a situation from victimizing to empowering, and I celebrate the turnaround.

This mindset is not something you learn and then never have to worry about again. It is a continuous effort of learning, applying, forgetting, relearning, and reapplying. After each success, soon thereafter life will present more challenging situations to test your dedication to this approach. Welcome these challenges with open arms. Each time you switch your mindset, you learn how to to do it sooner and more easily the next time.

It is like exercising. If you are out of shape and overweight and you decide you've had enough of that lifestyle, you change your ways and start working out. You walk more, you go for a jog or take fitness classes, and at first it absolutely blows butthole. Ugh, getting up in the morning and knowing you have to sweat and feel the pain of muscles growing can make it easy to skip it, choosing an excuse that may feel good in the moment but that is damaging to you in the long run. So, you stick with it. Occasionally, you have a setback and hit snooze, but you don't let that destroy the whole effort. Tomorrow, you try again. In the beginning, the temptation to rely on excuses will pop up often. The more you say no to the excuses, the sooner your brain will realize you are committed and it shouldn't bother trying to convince you otherwise. Once you adopt a no-excuses attitude, you stop trying to self-sabotage. Eventually, exercise becomes a habit, and something interesting happens. You notice that it makes you feel good. On days when you don't exercise, you feel like something is missing. It becomes a habit, and you start to look forward to the discomfort of pushing yourself.

Now, do you just stop working out? Fuck no! To keep it up, you have to keep working. The difference is that you've overcome the hurdle of getting to the level of fitness you wanted, which is the hardest part. The maintenance is the fun part. Exercise has become a part of your life and identity. Sure, some days you will fall for an excuse not to put on your running shoes, but you know you will get back on it tomorrow. You may continue to push yourself and try new workouts to keep you challenged, or you might keep doing your usual routine. Whatever works for you. The important thing is that you made a positive change, it became a habit, and it became part of how you function. You are a person who enjoys breaking a sweat, rather than someone who only sweats when it's hot out.

Learning to completely change the meaning you give difficult moments will be a similar journey. In the beginning, excuses will be frequent. Self-doubt at each failed attempt to take one hundred percent responsibility for your reaction will try to shake you from your efforts. Three words: Compassion, patience, and resilience. You forgive yourself, reflect on what you could have done differently, and try again. Pretty soon, you will reach a tipping point that propels you into the no-excuses attitude zone. You will find that looking at how the present moment is in fact happening for you is your new way of thinking. It becomes a habit, and after some time, it becomes who you are. Keep with it, let it go when it doesn't go as planned, and the next time you face difficulty or some negative response like anger, fear, frustration, or self-pity, try to switch your attitude a little sooner than the time before. With enough practice (and there will be plenty of opportunities to practice), it won't take as long and won't be as hard.

What do you have to lose? You've been living your life a certain way to this point. Are you willing to try something new? Give it a shot for just one month. Start today. Simply catch your response to some unforeseen problem or frustration and decide to actively search for the benefit, the gift, the lesson, or the humor. Attempt to swap expectation for appreciation. If after one month it still doesn't feel right to you, that's fine. You have my permission to go back to thinking you are the victim of whatever crap happens to you. It is always your choice. But choose wisely. This is your life, and by transforming your mindset you can make it outstanding. It's up to you, boo.

JET LAG TOOL KIT
HOW TO OWN YOUR SHIT

1. **Take accountability for your life.** Focus on how life is always happening for you, not to you. Apply this to your past, present, and future.
2. **Swap expectations for appreciation.** When things don't go as planned, switch your focus to gratitude for what went well, instead of where things fell short.
3. **See problems as opportunities to grow.** Practice changing your attitude toward one of empowerment and gratitude. You always have the power to choose your reaction. Make a choice that serves you and your greatest life.

4. **If you need a vent sesh with a friend, be on high alert to make sure it does not become a habit.** Occasionally is fine, but if that is your go-to response anytime something in life doesn't go your way, you run the risk of becoming a burdensome martyr. Vent by putting pen to paper and getting that fuckery out of your head with a good old-fashioned rage-write.

CHAPTER ELEVEN
DRIVE

INTENTIONAL FOCUS

"Where focus goes, energy flows."

TONY ROBBINS

How often do you think about your goals and dreams? What do you focus on each day? If you're like most of us, your vision is short-term. You focus on just getting by. Workin' for the weekend, like Loverboy. Your immediate goals and tasks consume your time: that big project you have to finish for work, what you will cook for dinner, how you were wronged by your coworker or friend, the never-ending to-do list. You must prioritize your time so that each day you give yourself the gift of long-term focus. Remember *why* you're in the daily grind and what you're working toward. What do you really want in life? Who do you want to be? What do you want to contribute? It's so easy to get caught up in the immediacy of tasks and forget that there is a huge difference between urgent and important. If you only focus on the short-term demands of your life, the long-term priorities will not get the energy and attention they need in order to happen.

This isn't to say that you should neglect the small but important things that consume most of the day. Rather, examine why you are doing each of these things and ask how they get you closer to your long-term goals and dreams. If your long-term vision is always at the forefront of your mind, you'll accept or decline opportunities or obligations based on whether they support that goal.

In the United States, many of us wear "busy" as a badge of honor. Someone asks you how you've been, and your auto-response is, "Busy, but good." What kind of bullshit answer is that? We see being busy as being hard-working, significant, important. If we continually focus on how busy we are, we will continue to do things to make us busy, like saying yes to things we don't really care about or things we feel obligated to do, or taking on more than we can handle. We will confuse being busy with having purpose.

The most valuable asset we have is time. How are you spending it?

Is your time being spent in a way that supports a positive focus or a negative one? Are you using up your time in areas where it isn't absolutely necessary? Examine all the tasks that take up the hours in your day. The 80/20 Principle (also called the Pareto Principle) states that in nearly all situations, approximately eighty percent of the effects are a result of twenty percent of the causes. What twenty percent of tasks are taking up eighty percent of your time? What twenty percent of tasks will give you eighty percent of the results you want? Believe it or not, the purpose of your life is—*gasp*—*not* to be busy. Free up your life to allow more time to focus on your big-picture goals by learning which tasks you can either eliminate or do more efficiently.

Keep in mind that when people first start out in their careers, it can be incredibly beneficial to say yes to every opportunity. Doing so opens doors, introduces you to new people and experiences, and helps you build momentum. However, once you are more experienced and established, you must be protective of your time. It's not about saying no to everything, but about being selective about what you take on. Maintain a mentality of "HELL YEAH" or "No." If an opportunity arises that doesn't pique your curiosity or seem like a chance for growth, it might be a good idea to let it pass so you have the bandwidth for an opportunity that makes you say, "HELL YEAH!!" By saying no to the good, you'll be able to say yes to the great.

Before you continue, take a moment to audit your time:

1. Notice where your time typically goes each day. What are the tasks that shape up an average morning, afternoon, and evening?
2. Apply the 80/20 Principle to your current schedule. Look for the tasks that take up eighty percent of your time, but only offer a twenty percent return on your goals. Shift your focus and energy on the twenty percent of tasks that produce eighty percent of the results. Locate opportunities for efficiency and improvement.
3. Prioritize part of your morning or evening (ideally when you first wake up or just before bed) to focus on long-term goals and dreams. Knowing what you are working towards and why it matters to you will help you become aware of available opportunities that will help you to achieve it.

If you're swamped and feel like you can barely keep your head above water, then this is even more important. Take time to free up your schedule. After all, time is the most valuable thing you've been gifted with. Prioritize and use it wisely. Don't just spend your time, invest it in ways that will prevent you from looking back with regret.

GOAL SETTING

"The greater danger for most
of us lies not in setting our
aim too high and falling short,
but in setting our aim too low
and achieving our mark."

MICHELANGELO

One of the greatest yet least-used tools we've been given as human beings is the ability to manifest the life we want. Manifestation is the act of transforming a thought into a reality through visualization and action. For some reason it has been lumped into the airy-fairy, woo-woo category, its power discredited by an unfortunate misinterpretation of how it's done and the benefits it provides. Olympic athletes have tapped into the invaluable effects of visualization and manifestation for decades. To be fully prepared, it is not just about the body, but also, and often more importantly, the mind. Athletes physically train and practice diligently, and apply the same discipline and rigor to the training of the mind. They picture their perfect routine. They imagine each step, each movement, each reaction. They imagine flawlessness and perfection, over and over (and over) again until the ultimate success becomes habituated and deeply ingrained in their mind, body, and spirit. Then, when it's go-time, they are able to surrender into what they have practiced physically and mentally so many times before.

We can tap into this any time with anything we want. The key is to visualize your goal in detail and picture it completed. Let yourself feel the emotions you would feel if you succeeded. How would you act? What would that look like? Picture it as though it were already a memory. Clarity and repetition are crucial here. The more often you let yourself be in that place of accomplishment, the more familiar it will become. It will begin to guide your actions and thoughts so they are aligned with your goal. Be cautious though, as this is where a lot of people misstep, and one of the reasons visualization and manifestation has gotten a bad rap.

All too often, people think they are manifesting or visualizing their dreams just by thinking *I want such-and-such* (a house in the mountains, to make a million dollars, to start a business, etc.) and leaving it at that. Don't get me wrong, I believe thoughts can be incredibly powerful, and it's important to think positively. But for visualization to work, you must do three things:

1. **Don't just state your goal** (i.e., "I want to be a millionaire"), but visualize it. Picture it happening. Daydream about it. Imagine what it would look like and bring forth the emotions associated with that success. Let yourself feel it as though it were already done.

2. **Repeat, repeat, repeat.** Let this goal consume you. As often as you can, do step one. Enjoy it and let yourself feel the successes and gratitude of accomplishment as often as possible. Repetition will keep

it fresh in your mind and will get it ingrained in your core.

3. **Take action!** This is the step most people leave out, and it's probably the most important. A dream without a plan of action rarely comes to fruition. When you come up with tangible steps to take toward a dream, it turns into a goal. And goals will be accomplished if steps are taken and progress is made. You cannot depend fully on the power of thought. Thoughts need to be paired with action.

I believe life wants us to succeed. It wants to give us everything we want and need to thrive and live our best life. But to do this, we need to make an effort and show that we're serious about it. We need to do everything in our power to move toward our goals. Then, as with so many things, a balance will be created by allowing grace to step in and guide us even further. It's a blend of disciplined action paired with surrender and trust. Too much of either will limit our progress. Put in the work, then trust it will happen.

What are your goals and dreams? Don't wait until New Year's Eve to think of what you want in the future. Take the time to figure out all that you want in this life. When you're setting your goals remember not to limit yourself. Let yourself dream bigger-than-elephant-balls dreams. This can be a fun, eye-opening practice. Give yourself twenty minutes to write down everything you want over the next one, three, five, ten, or twenty years—over your entire lifetime. Think of it as the ultimate bucket list, with all the personal experiences, financial and professional accomplishments, and emotional and spiritual growth you hope to achieve. The biggest challenge in this exercise is to avoid limiting yourself. You might find that inner critic stepping in and telling you you're ridiculous and you could never do that. Tell that critic "Thanks for trying to protect me from disappointment, but I don't need you right now," then make that goal even crazier.

When I first did this exercise, one of my goals was to make at least $30,000 each month. My logical side stepped in, saying there was no way I could do that and not to be so unrealistic. I paused, said thanks but no thanks, then asked myself *Why not go bigger? Why set any limit on what I can achieve?* I was placing myself in a box of limiting beliefs, and for what? So, I updated my goal to: I make *at least* $100,000 each month doing what I love and making a positive impact on the world, and it *continues to grow* exponentially and effortlessly. Why the fuck not? Maybe it will happen and maybe it won't, but at least I know that I didn't limit the seemingly impossible.

As you make your master goals list, notice when you try to limit yourself or critique yourself. Thank it, let it go, then make that goal even BIGGER and CRAZIER. Have fun with it! Go nuts for twenty minutes as you write all your dreams down: the tangible, the intangible, the seemingly impossible. Do this exercise at least once a year, and as the years go by, remember to look back every so often at what you wrote down. You will be amazed to see how many of those "crazy" dreams you achieved.

CONSISTENCY IS KING

"We are what we repeatedly do."

WILL DURRANT

We live in an interesting and exciting time. The world is moving at an incredibly fast pace, and technology is drastically changing the way we live. Never has there been so much opportunity to pursue your dreams and transform an idea into a stream of income. The internet has enabled us to instantly connect with people all over the world. People can generate revenue in places where the economic situation seems hopeless. In Venezuela, people are teaching Spanish to students around the world through online tools like iTalki or Skype, and, as a result, can survive in a society with record unemployment rates. All over the world, people are working full-time jobs but feel driven to moonlight with their own Etsy shop, freelance copywriting gig, or coding position through contract-for-hire websites. It has never been easier to make bank doing your own thing. All it takes is an unrelenting drive. Fortunately, it is possible for everybody to cultivate that. It is not something that only some are blessed with.

We all know a person who seems to have their hand in everything, busting ass, working on multiple projects and ventures, always pushing forward. We separate ourselves from them, thinking they are a special breed, born with something we weren't. What we don't realize is that the drive and energy they embody is something we all have access to and can generate. It comes down to what you want and the habits you create to get it. What is your dream life? How would you be living? What would you have? How would you feel? What would you contribute to the world? What would you do if you knew you couldn't fail? Chances are there's a big gap between where you are and where you want to be. No worries. It all starts with defining what you want and recognizing where you are in relation to it. To get to where you want to go, you have to know your starting point. That helps you create the map you need to arrive.

The challenge is that we are all so exhausted from our daily grind of just making ends meet that we don't have the energy to believe that our goals are possible. Throughout history, people have been dealt a fistful of shit and yet have still been able to rise up against all odds and live unimaginably incredible lives. Lives of fulfillment, success, and positive impact. They pushed through, persevered, and believed with their whole heart that they could accomplish whatever they set their mind to. They adopted a no-excuses attitude and created habits that would allow them to live as they wished, and habits that promoted health, vitality, and energy.

Take a moment to think about your ideal life. What would it look like? What would you love to do, be, or create before you die? Don't limit yourself here. Dream big! Take two minutes to close your eyes and imagine this life.

Now, ask yourself what kind of person you would have to be to achieve that life. Make a list of values and characteristics you would need to embody. Maybe it's drive, health and vitality, growth, gratitude, intelligence, or creativity. Remember, we are what we repeatedly do. Behind every person is a set of habits and beliefs that shape who they are and what they do. What are the daily habits you would need to have to achieve the life of your dreams? Which habits promote energy, grit, and creativity? Which of your current habits are holding you back? We adopt unconscious habits all the time, and they stick because they provide us with some sort of reward. If they didn't, we wouldn't do them. However, these habits often contradict who we want to be and what we want to do.

Be honest in your answers and really give this some thought. Reflect on how you act, speak, and think day to day. Is there a gap between who you must be and what you must do to accomplish your dreams, and how you behave now? Are you currently living in alignment with the values and characteristics that will take you where you want to go?

Observe your entire day, looking for the habits you have adopted. Ask yourself how they're helping you, what benefit they are providing, and whether they are helping you accomplish your goals. You are likely doing a great deal of unconscious stuff that will sabotage your efforts to become the person you need to be to live your dream life. If you can shift these habits into ones that provide you with a benefit in alignment with your goals, then you will be on the fast track to success. The key is to make sure the new habit has a clear benefit. Once you recognize its reward, you must apply a no-excuses attitude and remove entirely the question of whether you will stick with the habit.

Typically, in the process of developing a habit there is a split-second question of whether you will actually do it. It is the immediate decision: Will you snooze or not, exercise or not, eat that delicious cookie at 2pm or not. If you commit to a no-excuses attitude, it takes the inner battle out of it. The task becomes easier, and the habit occurs automatically. Until the habit is formed, try to set yourself up for success by eliminating the option of questioning it. Put your alarm across the bedroom so you have to get out of bed. Lay out your workout clothes so you just put them on and go. Hide the cookies or put a big note on them that says, "Not today, motherfucker!"

With repetition, it will get easier. Each time you choose to go one way or another, it will get easier to go the same direction the next time. So, if you choose to snooze today, it will be easier to snooze tomorrow. Conversely, if you choose to get up as soon as the alarm goes off, it will be easier to do so tomorrow. Each time you take a step in the direction you choose, it will be easier to do it the next time. Consistency is king.

AVOID THE CRAB-GRAB

Resilience. Grit. Drive. These are the pathways to success. Being resilient is about having the courage to get back up again no matter how many times you fall, and to view rejection and failure as a benefit because they mean you tried and learned and are one step closer to succeeding.

To live a big life, you have to stay true to your core, dream big, and do whatever it takes to get there. If you are too focused on what people will think of you or too afraid of rejection, you'll limit yourself in a way that will guarantee future regret. When you are on your deathbed you will be faced with all the what ifs. The dreams you thought weren't possible will gather around and die with you. Those dreams were yours and yours alone.

We were all born with a song inside our heart desperately waiting to be sung. (I mean this figuratively, fortunately, because my singing voice has the potential to make ears bleed—seriously, it sounds like screaming cats). Our experiences and curiosities are the tools we need to live our purpose. By following your curiosities and passions, you will be guided to the path you were meant to be on. Follow your interests and see where they take you. This life is all about learning and growing in a way that enables you to be your best self, singing the song that you and you alone can sing.

To live your life fully and authentically while creating the greatest good is something only you can do. The pie in the sky dreams you so quickly shut down pop into your mind for a reason. To ignore them for fear of how people will judge those dreams, or because you fear failure or rejection, is the true failure. Tell fear to suck it. You are a resilient motherfucker who will not be limited by fear. To live out of fear is to live a half-life, and to your future self, the one on that deathbed, you owe the certainty that you gave it your all.

All of us were born with powerful, natural resilience. To become functioning people and learn to speak and walk, we had to be resilient. Unfortunately, most of us stopped practicing resilience as each year passed because we noticed how much it can hurt. We forgot all the benefits of getting back up and focused only on the pain of the fall. As a result, we tried to avoid falling at all costs. So, here's the deal: Just because you've spent your adult life avoiding the fall doesn't mean you can't change gears now. Resilience and grit are cultivated with practice. Every time you take a step toward your dreams and goals and end up eating shit, you have a choice. Do you give up, or stand up and try again? You will notice that the more times you stand up after a fall, the easier it becomes to do so. It is just like developing any other skill. Practice and consistency will help you progress along the learning curve, and it will become easier.

Every time you hear the word *no*, change the meaning you give it. *no* doesn't mean that you suck ass or that you should stop trying to achieve your goal. See *no* as a good thing. That *no* is awesome, because it was a necessary step to get you closer to the *yes* you are seeking. Accept it, learn from it, try again, keep going. The *no* is only worthless if you stop trying and give up before you reach the *yes*.

If you put yourself out there and commit to living life fully, then you will most likely feel liberated and scared shitless at the same time. It can be lonely, breaking away from the norm in hopes of living your best life. When you decide not to settle for less than your dreams, you begin a journey that requires immense drive, because you will need to withstand the loneliness of that climb. You will be criticized and judged for trying. Don't take it personally, just trust in yourself and keep going. Seeing you attempt to live your best life will cause people to reflect on the ways they are not living in line with their own dreams, and they will try to pull you back down to keep you on the same level. It's known as Crab Bucket Mentality: When a bunch of crabs are in a bucket together and one tries to climb out, escaping their fate as a crab cake, the other crabs will pull him back down to keep him with the group. Don't become a crab cake. Resist being pulled and live among the liberated.

You may be criticized and judged if you try. But guess what? You may also be criticized and judged if you don't. Might as well choose the option that rings true for you. The option that keeps you on the path toward a life that deathbed-you will be proud of. The option in which your dreams surround you, patting you on the back in awe of your incredible fight to achieve the seemingly impossible: a life in which you use your gifts to realize your dreams. Say fuck it to the judgements and know that how you view yourself and your purpose is what matters. If you keep fighting toward your dreams with integrity and conviction, you will achieve them. Don't get distracted by people on the sidelines. They aren't even participating in the race.

I noticed an interesting phenomenon when I shifted my focus from fear of judgment or rejection to the dreams I felt I had to pursue. When I finally stopped limiting my being in an attempt to fall in line with others' expectations, I felt free. I took baby steps in exposing parts of myself I had been too afraid to show. The more I showed my true self, the more the closest and most supportive people in my life opened up, too. They began to show authentic bits of who they were, bringing our relationships to a much deeper level.

By sharing my dreams, as far-fetched as they were, they began to feel more real, more possible. Friends began to share their own. The dynamic of our relationship transformed into one of support and empowerment. Granted, some friends reacted the opposite way, trying to crab-grab and pull me back down to the way I used to be. That was to be expected. That is where the practice of resilience became invaluable. Once again, I was faced with a choice. Do I expend my energy on those trying to hold me back, or surround myself with people who uplift me?

The higher you strive, the fewer the people who will support your rise. So, above all, you must depend on yourself as you push forward and continue on your path. If the loneliness makes you waver, look for others who have done what you are trying to do. Read articles or books, listen to podcasts or interviews, surround yourself with real-life examples of success and fulfillment against all odds. The people who have accomplished their dreams and are living their best lives have at least one thing in common: they were committed and resilient in their pursuit. The only person they had to convince of their dream's viability and validity was themselves, and once they did, there was no stopping them. Break from the norm. Do everything in your power to listen to your heart and act on what it is calling you to do. You will be amazed by what you can accomplish.

JET LAG TOOL KIT
HOW TO RESIST THE CRAB-GRAB
AND PURSUE YOUR DREAMS

1. **Write it down.** Make a list, putting your dreams and goals on paper. Use as much detail as possible. Don't limit yourself.

2. **Manifest and visualize.** Give yourself permission to daydream. Act like an Olympian and visualize your goal being accomplished. Picture it so vividly that you feel and believe it. Focus on the "why." Why do you want it? What would accomplishing it do for yourself and others?

3. **Repeat.** Visualize your goal often. The more you do it, the more deeply you etch it into your psyche. When you wake up, think of your goal. When you go to bed, imagine it done. Become obsessed with it and let the excitement of its achievement consume you.

4. **Take action.** Determine the steps you need to take to accomplish the goal. What kind of person do you need to become to achieve it? Is there someone else who has accomplished that goal already? Study

them. How did they do it? Seeing the success of others can remind you that it has been done and can be done by you, too. It is harder to be the first because you must pave the way. Look at others' successes as a path that has been cleared. Learn from their mistakes and observe their wins, then make it your own.

5. **Trust in the process.** Remember that life is still pretty fucking awesome even if you haven't achieved your goal yet. Enjoy the journey and remember that progress is happiness. Taking steps toward your goal and celebrating the wins will keep you going even in times of doubt. Remember that if you are trying, life will step in and meet you halfway (or more). Be open to grace and guidance. Life may take you off the path that you're sure is the only way to reach what you want, but you must trust it. It may be taking you somewhere greater than you could have ever imagined.

CHAPTER TWELVE
SETTING THE FOUNDATION

GOOD MORNING!

Your alarm goes off. Groggy, you hit snooze. It goes off again. Snooze. Back to sleep. Snooze. Repeat this cycle until there is no more time to snooze, and you are officially running late. Turn off your alarm, check your email, Instagram, Twitter, the guaranteed-to-be-shitty news. Jump out of bed, quickly get ready, there's not enough time to eat something healthy so you stop at a coffee shop and pay $10 for a delicious, sugary muffin and some caffeine. Work eight, nine, ten hours, come home exhausted, make dinner, help the kids/spouse/pet/whatever, lounge on the couch, watch TV while you browse social media, go to bed. Repeat Monday through Friday, week after week, year after year. Before you know it, decades pass, and you realize that all the dreams you had for your life are getting fainter and less tangible in your mind. Time flies by faster than a fart in a fan factory, and then you look back on a life spent in the daily grind with little to show for it. The dreamer inside you who begged for you to listen has stopped trying to be heard. You're out of time.

Each day you are given a blank slate. A fresh chance to get one step closer to your goals. From the moment you open your eyes, you can choose the attitude you want to embody and your primary objectives for the day. It doesn't matter what you did yesterday, last week, or last year. You can begin again the moment you wake up. What an awesome gift! The way you start your day sets the tone, not just for the next twenty-four hours, but for the life you will end up living.

I have a strategy for making the most out of a morning,

the most formative part of the day. I believe that following this strategy could provide you with the foundation you need to live your best life. A life that will not pass you by, leaving you filled with regret for what could have been. Now, I realize that many of you probably don't have much time to spare in the mornings. A lot of folks recommend morning routines that can take thirty, forty-five, or sixty minutes, and I understand that for most, that is not a reasonable expectation. So, do what you can. A ten-minute routine is better than no routine at all. Modify it to fit your life so you will actually do it. The example below can be tweaked or followed a la carte to fit your availability (or lack thereof).

The first hour of being awake has the potential to kickstart incredible momentum—or, alternatively, to set you back. Be protective of what you expose your mind to within that time frame. One of the best ways to start your day is with gratitude and intention. Your alarm goes off, and you are still half-asleep and eager to hit snooze just once (or many more times). Don't give into the temptation. If it helps, put your alarm across the room so you must physically get out of bed to turn it off. Then immediately practice gratitude for the day. It can be as simple as thinking the words *Thank you*, or you can think of things you are grateful for in that moment. Hint: Waking up is a good one. Your bed. Your home. Toilet paper. So often we overlook ordinary gifts because their commonplace nature makes them more predictable than a pumpkin spice latte and UGGs during fall. We don't miss them until they are taken from us, and then it is too late. Might as well appreciate them while we have them, because there are countless people who are not as lucky.

Give thanks for your health, your home, the people you care about, running water, electricity, being safe, having a job if you have one, having a car if you have one, having access to public transportation (whether or not you use it), your education, your sight, your hearing, your voice, your ability to move. Even if you have a crazy-busy day, you always have enough time to start it by saying *Thank you*. It takes two seconds but has an incredible impact on your wellbeing.

You know how people always say that time flies and are shocked to see weeks, months, years go by without them even realizing it? Time passes whether we want it to or not. I've found that to work in alignment with your goals you have to be clear on how you want to spend your time. Setting your intention involves thinking about how you want your day to go, what you want to accomplish, how you want to act, speak, and think, and what sort of impact you want to make. By reminding yourself of the ways you intend to honor the gift of this day, you keep your goals at the forefront of your mind and consciously (and subconsciously) take actions that support them.

Sometimes it is helpful to work backwards to come up with your intentions. Imagine that you had the opportunity to speak with your ninety-year-old self right now. What advice would they give you to help you live your life fully and in alignment with your dreams? Who would you have to be today to make them proud, and to make them feel that yours was a life well lived? What characteristics and values would you need to embody?

Your intention can be as simple as "Today I want to make

progress on my goal, to be my best self, and to make a positive impact on those around me." It doesn't have to be long and complex. It can be whatever you want it to be, and whatever rings true to you.

My intention changes daily, but for the most part, I use the following structure:

Today I surrender to life and love. I let go of my need to control and instead trust in life's magnificent plan for me. Enable me to move through my day in alignment with my values of gratitude, love, compassion, humor, generosity, growth, and drive. Enable me to be my best self—my authentic, open-hearted, playful, wild, joyful self. Remind me that life is always happening for *me. Thank you for this day.*

If I have some big presentation or meeting, I picture it going flawlessly. And I think of any other large tasks I want to accomplish so they are fresh in my mind.

Setting your intention can take less than a minute. You have time for that. At the very least, try it out for two weeks and see if it is something that could add value to your life. It has the potential to be a game-changing habit.

Waking with gratitude and an intention has the power to drastically transform your day and, if done consistently, your life. To further amplify the effects of these habits, dedicate an hour of power: Use the first hour of your day to feed and grow your mind, body, and spirit. The hour of power is intended to optimize your success through intention and meditation, exercise, and empowerment, and is a surefire way to rise above and kick ass. Meditating can be as simple as expanding on your gratitude list and intention, listening to a guided meditation, or just following your breath for five minutes.

It's not some airy-fairy, metaphysical thing only to be used by ripe-smelling yogis and crystal-loving hippies (not that there's anything wrong with that, as they would say on *Seinfeld*). Think of it as exercise for your mind. It gives you a bit of peace and calm before the chaos of your typical day. Beyond just exercising your mind, creating a habit of working out in the morning will help balance out a healthy body. Exercising releases endorphins and kickstarts your metabolism for the day. To get the most out of these habits, you must dedicate time to ensure your good health and vitality through exercise (mind and body), sleep, and eating well. It will keep you going for the long haul and enable you to accomplish your goals and dreams.

For the last leg of the hour of power, you can listen to an uplifting or inspiring video or podcast, read something focused on personal development, or write out your goals. Usually, I listen to a podcast or YouTube video as I work out or get ready for work (multi-tasking, yo). The hour of power doesn't have to be an exact hour. Sometimes it will be more, sometimes less. It is more about applying the concept of a daily ritual that betters you and keeps you moving forward. If we don't set aside time to focus on our goals and reflect on the person we want to be, before we know it we will be that ninety-year-old wondering how it all passed by so quickly.

Pausing to examine what you want to accomplish and

who you want to be forces presence. It shakes your awareness, causing you to notice that today, you have the power to make a change. To make progress on your goals. To feel happiness and gratitude for where you are now and to keep striving toward greatness. It is your responsibility to be the best version of you possible. It requires effort and dedication, implemented through consistent daily tasks that take you one step closer to becoming better. There is always room for improvement, and there is always time to appreciate where you are now. Finding that balance is the pathway to living your life fully and in a way that will make you proud. It all begins with how you choose to start the day. Carpe diem, baby.

JET LAG TOOL KIT
HOW TO KICKSTART YOUR DAY WITH PURPOSE

1. **Begin the day with gratitude.** The first thing you think when you wake up: *Thank you.* Thank the day for letting you experience it, and for everything you are grateful for in that moment.

2. **Get out of bed.** Sit up. Move. This will prevent you from giving into the temptations of snoozing and will kickstart your brain.

3. **Set your intention for the day.** What do you want to accomplish? What kind of person do you want to be? How do you have to act/think/speak to be your best self today? What impact do you want to make?

4. **Brush your teeth.** It helps wake you up and takes care of your butt breath.

5. **Make your bed.** It is low-hanging fruit of accomplishment. It triggers a response of pride and motivation in your brain by checking off the first task of your day.

6. **Stick with it for the long haul.** The above steps take less than ten minutes, yet make a lasting impact not only on your day, but your life. Consistent small actions have the potential to create lasting positive change.

Want to take it even further? Add the following:

1. **Exercise.** When you get your sweat on early in the day, it revs up your metabolism and puts you in a positive frame of mind. Set yourself up for success by placing your workout clothes on your dresser so you have no excuse to not get up and get dressed. New to exercise? It could be as simple as going for a ten- or twenty-minute walk. Just move your meat sack.

2. **Meditate.** This can be just ten minutes of extend-
   ed gratitude and intention or following a guided
   meditation or your breath. Taking a few minutes
   in the morning to let your mind find peace can
   greatly help with clarity and tranquility throughout the day.
3. **Write.** Morning Pages is an exercise created by
   Julia Cameron in her book *The Artist's Way*. Basically, at some point in the morning before you begin your daily grind, write three pages about anything you want to get whatever is on your mind,
   off your mind. The key is to just keep on writing.
   Let it flow, without letting your pen leave the paper. Chances are it will suck. Just relax. Sucking
   is good (that's what he said). It allows you to get
   all the worry, stress, frustration, and chatter down
   on paper so your mind is clear and ready to roll.
   If you dedicate yourself to this habit, you will no-

tice deep insights exposing themselves amongst the penned-out shit, insights that would otherwise have remained buried. Some consider this exercise to be a version of morning meditation. Whatever works for you, boo.

4. **Organize.** Create a to-do list of the tasks you want to accomplish. Mark the top three you feel you need to get done to feel the most productive (often these will be the tasks you least want to do and may even be procrastinating). Writing it out adds accountability, and it feels awesome when you get to check it off as done.

CHAPTER THIRTEEN
YOUR GUIDING COMPASS

LISTEN UP

Trust. It is one of the most important elements of any relationship. Without trust we can't fully connect and allow our vulnerabilities to present themselves. If trust is broken in a relationship, whether among lovers, friends, or colleagues, it can be detrimental. Trust can be rebuilt, but doing so can prove to be incredibly challenging. If we want the relationship to succeed, however, then we must restore it. But because it is so challenging, most people end relationships instead of putting in this work, and understandably so. If they were to focus on rebuilding trust, they would have to risk a hurt that has already once occurred.

There is also a relationship of trust between life and you as a person. All your hopes and dreams are dependent not only on you, but on life as well. Most of us refuse to trust that our dreams will ever become reality. If we allowed ourselves permission to fully believe that, we'd find ourselves in a hugely vulnerable position of risking severe disappointment. It's scary to let ourselves dream big because it means we can see what's possible for our lives and then risk not getting it. Disappointment can be debilitating. But until you allow yourself to believe in something so much it almost hurts, you will not fully commit to it. The fact that we can dream up a potential future of greatness means we are capable of achieving it. This requires a trust in life. A trust that if you put in the effort and work toward a dream, life will assist.

I'm sure in your life there have been countless disappointments. With each one you may have lost just a little more trust in life aiding you and your goals. With each bit of trust lost, both in relationships with others and the one between you and life, a small callus begins to form on your heart to protect you. We don't want to fall as hard ever again. Muting our hope to mute potential disappointment is futile. All it does is keep you from playing full out. What if those disappointments were meant to happen? What if they were there to test our commitment to our dreams? What if they were lessons we needed to learn to succeed and grow on our path?

You can't let disappointment embitter you. You can't let the pain it causes to break your trust in life. There is magic in believing. Now, I'm not saying if you just have a belief in something it will happen. Affirmation without action is just delusion. Instead, if you adopt a feeling of conviction—a deep, knowing belief that you will accomplish what you want, then you will act in any way you can to get it.

To recap:

Affirmation - Action = Delusion
Conviction + Action = Results

A component of conviction is trusting that life has your back and viewing disappointments as critical steppingstones that get you to where you are meant to go. Conviction is the unwavering belief that what you want will happen—that it's not if, but when. When you have conviction in a dream, it transforms it into a goal. The difference between a goal and a dream is just a matter of creating a step-by-step game plan towards its accomplishment. The only reason it won't happen is if you stop believing in it and, as a result, stop trying. So, you must trust in yourself.

Thought has enormous power when backed with action. If there is a shred of doubt, it will act like a thread from a sweater, slowly unraveling the entire thing when pulled. Trusting in life and all the experiences it presents is the second half of conviction. It will be an ongoing practice of falling, getting back up, learning, and moving forward without letting doubt mindfuck you. The moment we start building walls to protect ourselves from future disappointment is the moment we start to settle for less than we're capable of. To limit our being is one of the greatest disservices we can do ourselves.

Throughout your life, you have experienced ups and downs that were all meant to teach you something, to provoke growth. Your purpose in life is to grow, learn, love, and become the best version of yourself possible. Part of that means listening to that tiny voice inside of you, calling out for you to act on your deepest dreams. When we first come into the world, we know the basic truths of who we are and then promptly ignore them to fit in. It's our job to then relearn what we know deep in our core but have buried over the years. We must listen to our inner wisdom and contribute to the world in a way that is unique to us.

You may have silenced that inner voice so often over the years that you can't hear it anymore. But if you give it the opportunity to come out, you will hear its whisper. Each of us is creative. It is a part of being human. The first step in tapping into that creativity is to acknowledge its existence. Then, as you notice and appreciate it, it will grow. That innate creativity is part of your inner voice trying to guide you to live the life you were meant to live.

There is no one single path to a full existence. Every one of us has a distinct path. Let your inner voice and creativity be your compass. You will know when you're on track when you feel gratitude, joy, love, and integrity. When you're able to get your head out of your ass and into your heart you will be able to see and move with clarity and perspective. The more you pay attention to those responses, the more you will be attracted to situations that prompt them. Life doesn't have to be as hard as we think. If we pay attention to the lessons within the difficulties and actively search for the benefit in both the problems and successes, we learn that everything is for our greatest good.

I said earlier that if we're not learning, we aren't growing. But it's also true that if we're not growing, we're deteriorating. Stagnation is regression, transforming moments of potential growth into moments lost. This doesn't mean that you have to always go full bore without rest. Rest and relaxation are important on your journey because they let you recharge, which prevents burnout and lets you appreciate how far you have come. Just don't linger too long. You will know in your gut when it is time to move forward again. Sometimes the journey to becoming your best self may feel overwhelming and never-ending, so remember that progress is happiness. Even the smallest step forward is enough. It puts you further along than you were, and that is the only criteria for success. Appreciate progress. Celebrate the little wins. Learn from the disappointments. If you believe with conviction, put in the work, and trust in yourself and in life, it will happen.

1. **Put both of your hands on your heart and breathe deeply and slowly.**
2. **Think back over your life.** What is something you were always drawn toward? What interested you or resonated with you on a deeper level? What grabbed your curiosity?
3. **Ask yourself, "What are my unique gifts?** What am I meant to do in this world? How can I use my gifts to serve and contribute?"
4. **Listen.**
5. **Now, there's a good chance that nothing happened, and you just heard some hyper-critical crickets.** Let it go. Repeat the above steps and be patient and compassionate with yourself.
6. **If that still doesn't work, ask yourself, "If my inner voice were speaking up for me right now from a place of love and wisdom, what would it say?"**

7. **Another way to tap into your inner wisdom is to imagine that you had the opportunity to speak with your future much older, much wiser self.** Ask for your future self's advice. If you receive only silence, reframe the question to "If they had to give me advice, what would they say?"

CHAPTER FOURTEEN
LEARNING TO LISTEN

SPAIN

It was May 2005, and I had one week left of my year abroad in Barcelona. My dad and stepmom flew out to visit, and on one of our last nights, we went out to a delicious late-night dinner typical of Spanish culture. We finished up around midnight and I took a cab back to my apartment. The taxi driver missed my building and dropped me off about a block from the front door. *No problema*—I didn't mind walking. During my year there I had felt incredibly safe, no matter the time of day or night. Barcelona never seemed to sleep. I frequently saw families, young people, and wrinkly silver-hairs alike wandering the streets well beyond 11pm. My neighborhood was generally lively regardless of the time of day.

As soon as I shut the cab door, I felt the hair on the back of my neck stand up. A tightening started in my stomach, then spread throughout my body. It was such an immediate and intense physical reaction I couldn't help but pay attention. It was after I observed the physical sensations with curiosity that I looked up and saw a man stumbling out of a dark alley-way about twenty feet from me.

Oddly, it was one of the few times my neighborhood seemed to be empty and not loaded with people wandering home after a late meal. Not a soul in sight minus myself and the alley-man. I had to walk past the alley he was coming out of to reach my front door, but with each step I felt my stomach tighten further. Something was wrong, and my body was doing everything in its power to wake me up.

I passed the alley-man, who appeared to be fucked up on

drugs or booze or both. He smelled like piss and seemed disheveled and angry. As I picked up the pace, he began to walk behind me more quickly until we were walking side-by-side. I felt the urge to yell no though he had yet to do anything threatening. And yet every part of my being was telling me to shout. So, I did. Or at least I tried to.

"NO!" my mind told my vocal cords to say, in hopes of scaring off the alley-man. Much to my surprise, instead of the powerful NO I envisioned, out came a feeble, weak, shaky "Noooo." I was startled. For the first time in my life, there was a disconnect between my mind's direction and my body's response. He looked at me and laughed and got a little closer. Again, I tried to shout "NOOOO!" But an even more pathetic "Nooo" came out. More laughter from the alley-man. I was walking as fast as I could without running, and he was matching my pace. I had a choice to make. Do I fight him even though he has yet to attack? I had years of training in martial arts, Tae Kwon Do, kickboxing, and self-defense. But what are the odds of my body doing what I want it to when I can't even shout No? Do I run to the door and hope I can beat him there? My door key was one of those antique ones you have to jiggle and shake for it to work. Rarely was getting into my building a quick process.

During all these thoughts, time was passing fast and slow. I continued to speed up, he continued to get closer, looking at me with eyes that telegraphed violence and bad intent. I knew in my bones that he wanted to do me harm.

I decided to run.

I took off and sprinted the two-hundred or so feet to my

door, and he chased after me. He was about thirty feet behind me when I jammed the key into the door and sharply turned it. It worked on the first try. It was a large glass entryway door with a mechanism that slowed its close to prevent it from slamming. I entered and pushed the heavy, slowed door with all my might to lock it before he approached. Just as he caught up and reached his hand out to stop it, the door clicked into place. Shut and locked.

I ran toward the steps from the entryway up to my flat. Against my better judgement, I turned back and looked. His forehead and hands were pressed against the glass as he stared at me, smiling with wild, malevolent eyes.

LEADING BY EXAMPLE

Each of us was born with an inner knowing, an intuitive wisdom hardwired in us to help us to survive. Amazingly, the physical response to my intuition kicked in before I even saw the alley-man and considered him a threat. How did my body know? Behind the scenes, our mind and body are working every second of every day to keep us alive. They perceive external threats before we are even aware of them.

Thanks in part to the tech boom, many of us have become dependent on external conveniences for basic survival, allowing intuition to take a bench seat. For most of us, life has gotten pretty easy. Long gone are the days of hunting for food and avoiding being eaten by a predator. Daily life is comfortable. Knowledge is available at the tips of our fingers, making it more and more convenient to get information without absorbing what we learn. If we don't know the answer to something, we Google it. Quickly and easily finding answers causes them to be quickly and easily forgotten. We live in the age of convenience, but convenience always comes at a price many of us don't realize. It costs us the environment, our minds, our growth, the benefits of progress and hard work. Humans are incredibly adaptable, and we've begun to adapt to the comforts of the modern world. The more external stimuli, the harder it is to hear the inner voice. It has been hushed so many times we can hardly hear it at all.

Connecting with your intuition and inner wisdom is a practice. It becomes easier to hear it the more you listen. When it screams out in alarm about danger we're not yet aware of, it differentiates itself from our more typical anxieties and worries. It resonates through your core and creates a physical response stemming from the gut. It sounds the alarms, but if you choose not to listen, then it's all a waste. Even though we're living in a safer self-made bubble than our ancestors, we are by no means insulated from danger entirely. Nearly every day there is a news story about a mass shooting or natural disaster. Peril is so common that most of us don't think about it for more than the few moments it takes before the next horrific story takes its place. We've gotten used to the shock and destruction. It's a terrifying thought—being in the wrong place at the wrong time could cost you your life. It can feel overwhelming and dangerous to just be out in public or in a large group. It would make complete sense to opt for growing out your 'stache and pit hair and pursuing a reclusive hermit life, hiding from the world in hopes of survival. But to live in fear is to not live at all.

Fortunately, there is another solution. To counterbalance the worry and fear we are bombarded with in every headline, we need to take charge of our mind and what it is exposed to. Every ad, headline, show, and article grabs for our attention, and typically if it bleeds, it leads. Guard your mind with all your might. Be aware of the information you feed your brain both consciously and unconsciously. By guarding your mind, you can create a space for that inner voice to speak. It's not possible to completely isolate yourself from the never-ending stream of bad news, but a simple start would be to limit the amount of time you spend reading it. Limit your exposure to all the crap that brings you down. Surround yourself with uplifting and positive people, podcasts, articles, websites, and books. It's your responsibility to take control of what your mind absorbs. By limiting the bullshit, you'll create space for positivity.

Now, you're probably thinking *OK, cool, lady, that's all nice and dandelions and rainbows, but how is that going to keep me safe in a world where I could be shot going to school or work and the only thing I hear is that the planet is dying and we're beyond fucked?* It is so easy to feel hopelessly helpless right now. The earth is throwing worldwide natural disasters at us, trying to shake us awake to see all the damage we're causing. Yet most people don't seem to listen or care. Several of our leaders, corporations, and many individuals deny the effects we're having on the planet and its imminent doom. Short-term financial gain has been blinding people to the true cost of convenience. It feels like no matter how much noise a person makes, it's not loud enough to be heard. So how on earth can we not lose hope in such hopeless times?

By leading and living by example. Focus on what you can do as an individual. Be the change you want to see. It's much easier to change yourself than it is to try to change everyone else. Small actions can have big ass impacts, so never underestimate the positive effect you can have on the world. The best way to counterbalance overwhelm is to act.

Perhaps you feel like shit about the state of our planet. Fair enough. But feeling like shit and doing nothing about it doesn't do any good. It just creates more anxiety and leads to a lot of talking about what is wrong and expecting others to fix the mess. Instead, we must act.

What can just one person do in a world of nearly seven

billion people? Maybe it means you pick up one piece of trash a day. Maybe it means you stop eating meat from unsustainable sources. Maybe you start bringing your own reusable bags to the grocery store for produce. Don't do these things from a state of pissed off bitterness or self-righteous fuckery. Do them because you care about where you live and because it's the right thing to do.

This also applies to counterbalancing the hate we're bombarded with in our daily news. Be the change. Be the open-minded, compassionate individual the world needs to create dialogue with others that will open doors to commonalities instead of differences. Practice kindness. Practice integrity. Practice being patient and curious in situations of disagreement and misunderstanding. Extend unexpected kind and caring acts towards others, strangers and friends alike. Like I said, kindness is more contagious than herpes. It is an antidote to the anxiety that comes from being too focused on self. When you focus on what you can do for others you get out of the worry that clouds your head and instead enter your heart. Bending to the destructive will of fear just damages the world even more. You must choose love. That's how lasting change will occur.

So much of the strife you feel comes from being too much in your own head. We overthink interactions, questioning ourselves and others, get stuck in analysis paralysis, and ruminate over past hurts, wrongs, or mistakes to the point of exhaustion. When we have our head in our ass, everything seems shitty, making it difficult to be happy and enjoy the moment. We get caught up on past bias and beliefs and it disables us from seeing a situation with clarity and gratitude. The solution? Get out of your head and into your heart.

Connecting to appreciation is one surefire way to get into your heart. Thinking from the heart involves connecting to love, gratitude, and surrender. You let go of your worries and replace expectation with appreciation. Sometimes it is helpful to physically put both your hands on your heart and breathe deeply while you switch your focus to gratitude. By pausing and taking a few deep breaths, you give yourself a moment to be present. In that state, focus on something you're grateful for. This grateful presence is your natural state of being, but in the chaos of daily life we often forget how to connect to our core. When we get out of our head and into our heart, we can go from inner asshole to inner wisdom. When you get into your heart, you connect to love and appreciation for the moment at hand.

An excellent way to snap out of suffering is to focus on how you can help others. An amazing thing happens when we do a kind act for someone else—we get out of our head. We stop dwelling on our own problems and are forced to focus on something greater than us. By putting our efforts into helping the greater good—whether that be volunteering, picking up litter, holding the door open for someone, helping an oldie across the street—we are putting our energy towards connection. We suffer when we're too focused on ourselves. Anxiety, anger, resentment, depression, and sadness are all emotions that stem from a focus on self. They dissolve when we shift our attention to helping others. It forces you out of asshole-autopilot and gets you to see the bigger picture. By applying your time, money, or talent towards the betterment of a cause beyond yourself, your own problems fade in urgency.

Next time you are all up in your head, mulling over someone who hurt you or a situation where you feel like you really fucked up, perform a random act of kindness. Smile at a stranger, buy a coffee for someone anonymously, hold the door open with a smile. Just those tiny acts will awaken something inside you. Amplify the action and the reaction will grow exponentially. Kindness creates a ripple effect far beyond what is visible. A smile can go a very long way. Think of it as a good sort of selfishness. By being selfless and focusing on others, you are, in fact, helping yourself.

There is a guiding voice inside us that tells us what is right and wrong for each of us. This may be different from person to person. If you listen to it and act on it, it will continue to speak up more clearly and loudly and eventually you will see how much guidance you are able to receive in living your best life. Trust it. Listen to it. It knows what you have forgotten.

One of the ways to create enough space for your inner wisdom to speak is through meditation. There are countless methods practiced all around the world, and each person seems to have a specific style they consider to be the best. Guided, Vipassana, Mindfulness, Transcendental, the list goes on. Don't fall into the trap of thinking there is just one right way. Do what works for you. Meditation is wonderful because the only thing you need to do it is yourself. It is not necessary to go to a retreat or take an expensive course. It is not necessary to subscribe to a monthly app or have a fancy meditation room with incense. All you need is your mind. That's it. Totally free, totally simple. Sure, many of the above methods are great and a lot of people swear by their benefits, but please don't feel that to meditate properly you need external help.

A simple way to get started is just by following your breath. Focus on your breath going in and going out, then try to extend the amount of time it takes to inhale, hold, and exhale. Sitting with your eyes closed and focusing on your breath for just five minutes a day can make a huge difference on your mental clarity and strength. As thoughts come into your mind, just send them on their way without clinging or reacting to them. Return to your breath. In, out, in, out. Repeat this over and over again until the time you've allotted for meditation is complete. Gradually you can increase the duration and see the benefits grow exponentially.

If you've never meditated before, you might find five minutes to be impossible, as to-do list items race through your brain and past annoyances or frustrations bubble up. Quieting the mind may feel like an impossible task that's boring as fuck. Just remember, even though the concept is simple (just follow your breath) you are still learning a new skill. To improve any new skill, you must practice to improve.

If you are just starting out, it might be helpful to also explore guided meditations that can be found for free on YouTube. There is also a huge selection of apps that have free guided meditations. It is not necessary to pay to meditate unless you need the accountability to make you do it. Guided meditations can vary greatly. A good one to begin with is a gratitude-focused meditation. By focusing on what you are grateful for you will alter your mental state drastically. It's an instant mood booster.

Dedicating just a couple of minutes a day to yourself can provide overwhelming benefits for your mental wellbeing. It will create space for your inner wisdom to speak up. It will help create a protective barrier from all the outside negativity that each of us face on the daily. If nothing else, it will give you a few moments of undisturbed peace.

LIFE'S BEST TEACHER

Life is a funny thing. We often become so enthralled by our own personal melodramas that we lose focus on the bigger picture. Typically, it isn't until we're staring death in the face that we are able to see all the reasons things happened as they did. It is hard to get clarity in a situation when you are in it too deeply. You must detach and look at your life from a bird's eye view to understand daily life's grip on your clarity.

The one thing that is certain in life is that every one of us will eventually kick the bucket. It's guaranteed. The fact that we don't know when ironically blinds us to its gravity. Our mortality typically isn't at the forefront of our thoughts unless we encounter a situation that acts like a friendly little throat punch, snapping us out of our blissful denial. The death of a loved one, a close call during an accident, a decline in our health, a natural disaster, or a terminal diagnosis are the sort of reminders it takes for most of us to remember life's fragility.

So many of us move through life just going through the motions. So many wasted moments of worry, anger, or fear. If we could have just remembered that we all die and that suffering always passes. Problems are proof that we're living and should thus be cherished. Because the moment they don't exist is the moment we're six feet under.

Death is not to be feared. Rather, it should be appreciated and viewed as one of the best teachers we have. Death is life's way of reminding us to live. I'm not advising a crazy blow-all-your-savings last hurrah because you could die at any moment. Rather, I'm suggesting that you find a balance between long-term planning and short-term living. Use death as a reminder to let go of the worry, anger, pain, and sadness that keep you from enjoying the moment. Learn from them and let them go. With a broader perspective, so many of the problems you experience will seem more like gifts than grievances. Step back and observe the problem with the detachment that comes from realizing that in the grand scheme of your life this is just another fleeting moment that makes your experience here a little spicier.

Today, after putting down this book I ask that you watch the world with glittering eyes. Look at the crazy miracle of us all being on this planet together, spinning at a thousand miles per hour in the middle of a vast and infinite universe. Look with justifiable awe at the earth's incredible beauty and the mind-blowing inventions of mankind. Reflect on the almost purposeful randomness of our intertwining lives, and know that because it could all go away in an instant, it is precious. Every person has a unique story and is in the process of learning and growing as we all mesh together on our journeys. Think about some of the relationships in your life today and how unlikely it is that you would ever meet that person. Your lives intersecting at the exact moment they needed to for you to form a friendship comes to seem nearly impossible. And yet it happened.

Move through today with death at the forefront of your mind. Don't wait until your final moments to allow yourself the opportunity to appreciate life. Let compassion and gratitude guide you. Keep an open mind and an open heart as you encounter unexpected situations, and remember that when you replace expectation with appreciation, your whole life will change. There is a benefit in every single moment. The key to finding them is to actively search for them. Look for the lesson, the gift, the good, or the humor, and you will find it. Do the best you can, and you will avoid future regret by knowing you gave it your all. Get busy living.

JET LAG TOOL KIT
HOW TO KEEP UP HOPE IN A SEEMINGLY HOPELESS WORLD

1. **Be aware of what you are exposing your mind to.** Watch out for negativity you may be subconsciously welcoming into your life through social media, news, websites, podcasts, radio, and articles. Set a cap on the amount of time you allow yourself to be exposed to the non-stop shitshow in the news.

2. **Invest all that awesome time you save from limiting your exposure to bad news in something better.** Boost your positivity and empowerment through podcasts, books, and articles that are uplifting and educational.

3. **Be the change you want to see in the world.** Lead by example. Remember that small actions can have big ass impacts.

4. **Give yourself at least five minutes a day to just be.** Focus on your breath or do a guided meditation. Attempt to clear your head for at least five minutes a day.

5. **Try to listen to the inner wisdom and intuition inside you.** It's always there. By consistently following the above steps you create room for it to come to the fore. The more you listen, the more clearly it will speak and be heard.

CHAPTER FIFTEEN
SEEING THE MAGIC

CUBA

Roberto's tanned, weathered hands expertly rolled the dried tobacco leaves into the quintessential Cuban cigar. Sealed with local honey, the cigar was set aside to dry as Roberto grabbed another resting in a box on the table. He began the process of cutting the cap and lighting it. He and his family ran his tobacco farm in Viñales, Cuba, for decades, recently opening it up to tours for travelers looking for an authentic experience from a seasoned farmer. Roberto spoke of the changes in Cuba over the last couple of years. Life in Viñales was simple and slow-paced, in the best way possible. Shifts in the political climate did not bother him. He just went with the flow and prioritized what was important to him. He focused on working hard, providing for his family, and spending time with his loved ones. That was his recipe for happiness. Along with several home-grown and hand-rolled cigars smoked throughout the day, of course. It seemed to be working—there was a look in his eyes as he spoke, his hands effortlessly rolling cigars. A look of pride, gratitude, joy. It was a look I have come to notice more in countries termed "developing nations" than in my own.

Over the last couple of years, a lot had changed politically between Cuba and the United States, and Americans had recently been permitted to visit Cuba if in accordance with specific travel purposes. I had obtained a general license under the people-to-people exchange category along with four other friends eager to experience the rawness of a culture not yet tainted by mass American tourism. It did not disappoint.

We rented rooms within the homes of locals and after

traveling outside of Havana, found exactly what we were looking for. In an era of constant bombardment of the internet, advertisements, and social media, Cuba was a breath of fresh air. It was the first time since the internet became so prevalent in our daily lives that I had zero access to it for ten days. The pace of life was slower. People seemed to appreciate togetherness. In parks, on the street, in restaurants, people engaged with one another. If they were by themselves, they engaged in their environment, observing it with curiosity and reflection. People were not chained to their screens. They were aware of what was happening in front of them, seemingly present without the deep effort we strive for in Western culture. In the United States, presence and mindfulness have become buzzwords that we struggle to embody and apply. Countless books, courses, articles, and seminars purport to teach presence and mindfulness, yet in Cuba, it seemed to simply be a way of life.

People walked down cobblestone streets talking with one another and looking around, aware of their surroundings, saying hello to folks they didn't even know. Wishing them *buen provecho* in restaurants, smiling at passersby, acknowledging others as opposed to ignoring them like I've grown accustomed to in the U.S. It supported a common theme I had noticed on my travels to developing nations—it seemed like the lower the population, the more connected they were to family, friends, even strangers, and, perhaps as a result, the happier they were (mo' money mo' problems?). It seemed counterintuitive, considering so many of us base our entire lives on achieving success in the form of accomplishment, accumulation, and consumption. Maybe we've been going about it all wrong. Maybe we've missed the point.

What people lack in possessions and money they often make up for in relationships with friends and family. Cambodia, Nepal, India, Bolivia, Guatemala, Cuba—so many of the countries that I've traveled to that face record poverty and unemployment levels, unimaginable corruption, substandard healthcare, and limited education have some of the strongest familial relationships I've ever seen. Family and friends are invaluable. Connection with others creates a sense of community in a society neglected by its government. In the most difficult times, when things can feel overwhelming and hopeless, to know you are not alone can be the one difference between surviving and thriving. When people don't have much, they tend to place greater emphasis on the things that truly matter. Connection, love, community, togetherness, generosity, compassion, humor, creativity, resourcefulness—these are the keys to making it in even the direst situations. And in areas of the world where things aren't as dire, they are the keys to living a life of meaning. They add depth to success, and when placed at the forefront of one's values, they create a sense of fulfillment.

Throughout our time in Cuba, we noticed the people seemed to emanate joy and appreciation. Cuba was music. Laughter. Conversation. The rumble of a 1950's Bel Air. The soundtrack of this country was all-encompassing—it filled your body with a vibrant energy. But on the seventh night of our trip, Fidel Castro passed away, and the morning after it was as though someone had abruptly turned down the volume. Silence and solemnity filled the air.

After our time in Viñales, we arrived in Trinidad the day prior to Castro's death. The charming city grabbed hold of my history-loving heart immediately. Its past was prevalent everywhere you looked, from the cobblestone streets and the quaint town squares to the aging walls of our *casa particular*—all dating back hundreds of years to when it was a bustling colonial town. As with much of Cuba, its history and present shared common ground. The deteriorating and shadowy walls of the early-18th century *Iglesia de Santa Ana* were brought to life by the sound of young boys playing *fútbol* within the poorly padlocked doors.

That day we explored like others did: mojito in one hand, occasionally petting the friendliest street dogs ever with the other. Nearly everywhere we went, music was playing, and people were taking full advantage of the moment—laughing joyously and dancing on the cobblestone streets. I chose to partake in the laughing rather than the dancing...it's been noted on multiple occasions that I can eat salsa much better than I can dance it. The day passed quickly and slowly, like travel days tend to do. We eventually called it a night, only to wake up the next day to a completely different city.

We awoke to an outstanding breakfast on our *casa particular's* outdoor terrace. It was $5 for coffee, tea, fresh mango juice (my ultimate weakness), eggs, ham, tropical fruit, toast, crepes, and, surprisingly, breakfast cookies. When we were mid-feast, Maryoley, the *casa's* owner, walked up to us with a grave expression. She told us that Fidel Castro had passed away very early that morning. It was one of those moments in which time stood still and the importance of the event made your hair stand on end. The country would be in mourning for nine days. No banks. No music. No fiestas. No sale of alcohol. Maryoley began to tear up as she said they lost their hero and walked in a daze back to her room. The breakfast cookies lost their appeal almost immediately.

The soundtrack of Trinidad was replaced with the murmur of countless television sets playing footage of Castro throughout his life. No marketplaces were set up, and even the street dogs seemed somber. Since we only had one night left in Trinidad, we decided to spend the Saturday evening wandering the silent streets. The echo of horse hooves clomping against the cobbled roads paired with the dim amber lights made it far too easy to imagine life when Trinidad was a bustling pirate town in the 1500s.

The Sunday following our magical Saturday night of solitude, we left for Santa Clara, where we would spend our last night before heading back to the United States. After settling into our *casa particular*, we wandered the streets and were surprised to see the buildings surrounding Parque Vidal being cleaned with rushed determination. Exterior walls were scrubbed and painted, windows washed, and plants trimmed. The city was preparing for the nationwide procession honoring Castro that would begin the next day.

The following morning, after indulging in another breakfast feast, we walked back to Parque Vidal only to see thousands of people lined up around the blocks waiting to offer their condolences. People of all ages stood in a seemingly endless line that wound throughout the city center, many holding flowers and photos of Castro. The strong sense of national community was unlike anything I'd ever seen. And yet the general opinion of Castro varied widely. He was loved or hated depending on how his decisions affected a person. It was a reminder to keep an open mind and recognize that the impact of circumstance changes from person to person.

I returned to the United States with a feeling of reverse culture shock and immense gratitude for having witnessed such a raw version of Cuba. People seemed more connected to each other than to their phones. Although they didn't have much, everyone cared for and appreciated what they had. Their resilience let them view the twists and turns of life with humor and connectedness. And if all else failed, they would tell us that "a little Vitamin R" seemed to help (their charming euphemism for rum).

It was a reminder to reflect on our priorities and appreciate what is truly important. What are we working for? What are we living for? Sometimes we get so caught up in the motions of working, earning, and consuming, that we forget to pause to ask ourselves why. In societies of abundance, we often overlook the gifts we have been given. We tend to take for granted our relationships with our loved ones and the comforts of our daily lives. If we strip away all the distraction, we might be able to see that we have similar priorities as Roberto. To take pride in what we do, appreciate what we have, and love the ones we are with.

YOUR MOST POWERFUL TOOL

Gratitude. Perhaps that is the most important key to living a life of fulfillment and not being an asshole in daily life. When we acknowledge all the beauty around us, it creates a ripple effect of abundance. The more we notice what life has given us, the more it presents itself. Gratitude creates an immediate connection to the present moment. It forces your attention to the gifts in front of you and draws you into the now. With a bit of reflective appreciation sprinkled throughout your day, you will notice the magic around you.

Gratitude is a surefire way to create presence and mindfulness, and it enables you to pause briefly to take a mental snapshot of what is going on around you. By appreciating whatever is happening and viewing it as a gift, you're subconsciously creating awareness for that moment. There is always something to be grateful for. You can always see what is wrong in a situation, but you can also always find what is right. It's a choice. Choosing to see what is going well and actively searching for the gift, the lesson, or the humor is what will create a lifetime of memories that feel fully lived.

We tend to get accustomed to things going well—the average, daily occurrences that go as planned barely make an impression on us. Clean water coming through the faucet, electricity at the flip of a switch, heat from the press of a button, hot water, the internet, having a phone, having enough food to eat. Most Americans have been blessed with so many things that an astonishing portion of the world has never experienced consistently or even at all. Just waking up in a bed and knowing that outside is safe as opposed to war-torn is a luxury. Because these gifts feel so common and reliable, we tend to discredit how amazing they are. In a practice of gratitude, it is crucial to appreciate and acknowledge the little as much as the big. They would surely be missed if they weren't a part of our lives. So, marvel at the seemingly ordinary.

When you choose gratitude over expectation, you're more inclined to trust in life's flow. By being grateful for whatever comes your way, you will notice a pattern of situations and events that have been put before you as an opportunity to grow and learn. Some events may have seemed like a cluster-fuck at the time, but looking back, you now realize that they led you to where you were meant to be. Take a moment to think about that.

What is one moment in your life that seemed so horrible, so painful, that you barely got through it? Now try to follow the chain of events after that moment. What did it lead you to do, change, think, and feel? What did that event disrupt in your life or in your being that has brought you to where you are now? As I mentioned, it is always possible to find the negative in each situation, but the positive is equally available. There is a benefit in everything we experience. It is our job to find the good, the learning experience. To see the magic. It is always there—you just have to look for it.

Start to integrate a habit of gratitude in your daily life. Begin and end each day with appreciation. As soon as your alarm goes off think of three things that you are grateful for. Chances are in your pre-coffee state they will be as elaborate and profound as *I'm grateful for my pajamas. I'm grateful for toilet paper.* Hey, that works! To be grateful for the little, common blessings is just as beneficial as appreciating the larger things. In the evening when your head hits the pillow once again, think once more of three things you are grateful for. If you need help narrowing it down, choose from your experiences that day. What went well? What made you smile? What did you do that you were proud of? The more you recognize moments of gratitude the more you will live in a state of appreciation, seeing how every experience, the good and the bad, is a moment of grace.

If we are open and receptive to the present moment, we can achieve a state of appreciative observation for all that is unfolding before us. To be open is to think with one's heart instead of one's head. When we are too much in our head, we start analyzing every little thing and labeling it as something that we like or dislike. Developing the muscle of choosing the positive reaction takes practice, but just like any new endeavor, it will get easier the more you do it. With enough repetition it will become second nature, a habitual response that can drastically transform your life.

Being receptive to the present moment involves a great deal of vulnerability. It exposes us to potential pain and hurt. I used to consider vulnerability a weakness, but I realized that when someone chooses to be vulnerable, they are staring potential hurt in the face and risking it anyway. That is not weakness, that is strength. It is courage. Being gratefully openhearted enables us to live a big life—to go all in. Enough of standing along the sidelines with a protective barrier surrounding our hearts! It is time to break down the walls we've built up and liberate our authentic selves. Again, the barriers we think are protecting us are actually harming us. The sooner we realize that the sooner we can be free. It may be scary, but many of the moments in which we feel most alive come with fear or potential pain. So, it comes down to the lifelong act of choosing love in the face of fear.

If we break down low-energy emotions like anxiety, overwhelm, doubt, anger, frustration, or resentment, we can see that these are all rooted in fear. The age-old fear of not being or having enough. This fear can make us act in ways we are not proud of and that are the opposite of our true nature. It is during those moments we must lean into love and vulnerability through gratitude.

Gratitude is the knife that cuts through fear with ease. It is the remedy, the antidote. In times of fear, place both hands on your heart and recall a moment when you felt incredibly grateful. It could be from yesterday, last week, last year, your childhood, whenever. Imagine that moment as if you were there looking through your own eyes. Let the feeling of gratitude consume you. Feel it spreading over you and enveloping you. Visualize the moment in vivid detail. Breathe deeply, and then let it all go. When you completely focus on gratitude, you free yourself from the grip of fear. They cannot exist simultaneously.

Moments that compel us to react in anger, sadness, pain, or fear are there to test us. They are opportunities for learning and remembering that there is always more than enough. You are enough. You are made up of love in your core. Love and gratitude are infinite resources that can never become scarce.

All that needs to change is our perception. We must remove the mask of fear and view life through our heart. Our authentic core is made up of a common thread that connects all of humanity; the love we crave exists within us, and the more we express it, the more freely it flows.

Many of us fall into the trap of thinking that the moment we are grateful for something, life will pull it out from under us and take it away. So, we avoid fully appreciating the thing we love most out of fear that we will lose it. But muting joy or gratitude does not prevent pain. All it does is keep you from living fully and truly enjoying what you've been given. Gratitude begets more gratitude. Don't futilely attempt to protect yourself from potential pain by not appreciating all that you have. Don't give into the temptation of fear-based scarcity thinking. Embrace the vulnerability of openhearted gratitude, and you will cultivate pure joy for all that is.

1. **Breathe deeply.** Fill your belly with air in a slow, deep breath. Exhale slowly. Do this at least three times. Just taking the time to breathe deeply can help you to pause for a moment and feel present and grateful. If nothing else, it will calm you.

2. **Look around and notice at least one thing you are grateful for.** Think about how lucky you are that it is here in this moment and what had to go right for it to be here.

3. **Close your eyes and think of a moment in your life that you are truly grateful for.** It could be from whenever: yesterday, last week, last year, your childhood. Imagine the moment in detail and remember what it was like as though you are there now. Think of what each of your five senses experienced in that moment. Breathe it in and give thanks. Let yourself feel it as though you are there now. Feel it fully.

4. **Get a piece of paper and a pen and make a list of everything you are grateful for.** This could be in general, specific to this day or moment, or to a particular person. Just the act of writing it down cultivates a sense of gratitude.

5. **Smile.** Even (especially) if you don't feel like it. The concept of "fake it 'til you make it" really works. Stick with it for a couple of minutes

6. **Think of someone you know and wish them joy, happiness, and love.** Wish them well. You can also do this for people you know neutrally or not at all. You can even do this for people who have wronged you. This is a version of loving-kindness meditation (Metta meditation), which involves wishing wellness to someone you care about, someone you know but not particularly well, someone you don't know at all, someone who you feel has wronged you, and to yourself.

By building up to the person who has wronged you it enables you to dissipate the feelings of hurt. Eventually the feeling of wellness for them will grow to be more than just words and will be genuine.

7. **Get outside, even if it's colder than a witch's tit or hotter than the devil's gooch.** Being in nature recharges us.

8. **Do something kind for someone.**

9. **Practice an act of openheartedness.** Smile at a stranger, ask someone how they are doing, hold the door for someone, or just let someone merge ahead of you while driving instead of flipping them the bird.

10. **Put your hands on your heart and breathe.** Give thanks for your heart and all that it has guided you to do. Or just give thanks for the fact that it is beating!

People are always searching and striving for joy, and they think that once they are joyful, they will be grateful. But the opposite is true. Feeling gratitude is what leads to joy, and that joy leads to further gratitude, igniting an incredible loop of two powerful emotions.

CONCLUSION
BON VOYAGE

> ## "It is no measure of health to be well adjusted to a profoundly sick society."
>
> JIDDU KRISHNAMURTI

Let me introduce you to an unfortunately common interaction in today's culture:

> Person A: "Hi, how are you? How have you been?"
> Person B: "Pretty good. How about you?"
> Person A: "Oh, same ol' same ol'. Doing fine."

Barf! Ok, I know that this is just a basic conversation, and it would be a little intense to respond to a friendly "How are you?" with a 30-minute play-by-play of your recent work melodrama or family strife. But let's be honest. For most of us, these dull responses are a more genuine reading of how we are feeling and the life we are living than we care to admit. We have gotten sucked into the monotony of averageness. The daily grind of just getting by and going through the motions is resulting in a life not lived fully.

You were meant for more. When is the last time you felt better than good, fine, or okay? When is the last time you felt great? Or dare I say, outstanding?

We have settled for The Okay…The epitome of ass-hole-autopilot.

Here's the deal: You get what you tolerate. If you tolerate day in and day out of just being "fine" peppered with a rare "awesome" then that is what you will get. You've drawn a line in the sand for what you are willing to endure, and for most of us, that line is being just okay or good. Fine has become comfortable and common. You may believe that's just the way it is simply because it's what you're used to. But let your eyes drift to the quote above. Just because you fit in with what is considered normal among your peers, your family, and your community does not mean that it is how it should be. There *is* another way to go through life: the way you are meant to live.

Again, you get what you tolerate. Pause a beat and let that sink in again. Where you are right now—how you feel, how you live, the relationships you have, the experiences you face—are all based on the conscious and subconscious standards you have set for yourself. If you think that the best case for your life is to be decently comfortable and feel pretty good most of the time, then guess what? That is about as good as it will get until you decide that you can have, feel and be more—much more.

Sure, even if you set your standards super high, you will occasionally have down days. Shit happens. But it is a higher level of shit, because you decided that you do not tolerate low level turds. You will not let life's unforeseen figurative anal blowouts hold you back because you know your life is better than that. You will not tolerate the stranglehold that negative belief systems have over most of us. The "doing good/fine" peeps will see problems as excuses that reinforce their current situation and attitude. The "doing freakin' awesome" folks will see those same problems as opportunities to grow and see the gift in even the nastiest of crap. They will know to their core that this too shall pass and that nothing will keep them from their higher standard of living.

If you tolerate unhealthy relationships in which you are unappreciated and taken advantage of, then you will frequently find yourself in those kinds of relationships. If you tolerate a job where you are drained, demeaned, and miserable, then that is the exact work environment where you will find yourself clocking in Monday through Friday. If you tolerate an income where you are just scraping by and never seem to have enough, then you will be constantly facing that financial scarcity. If you tolerate a lifestyle where you're out of shape and unhappy with your body, then that is the way you will live. If you tolerate a mindset of victimhood in which you believe you do not have the power to change your attitude or your life, you are destined for a life of responding like Person A and Person B.

Fuck. That. Shit. Raise your standards. Change your life.

Enough is enough. No matter where you are in life, you always have the power to change. Don't just draw a line in the sand. Draw a line in the wet cement. Decide once and for all that you've had enough of mediocrity. You will not spend your life tolerating less than you deserve. You will take control of your ability to choose. To choose an attitude of empowerment and gratitude. To recognize that it is up to you, and you alone, to determine what you are willing to tolerate. It is time to raise your standards. Tell good/fine/okay to suck it.

Resolve to live the amazing life you were born to live. It all starts with a single choice to see things differently. To see that every situation in your life and your interpretation of how it affects you is up to you. Are the problems holding you back? Or are they acting as fuel to propel you forward? Are you committed to learning and growing and seeing the gift in a problem no matter how badly it hurts? Are you willing to go all in? To go through life with conviction that you were meant to live an awesome, fulfilling, joyful life? A life where you are just so grateful you can't help but see that everything is happening to push you forward and make you even better? This all starts with a decision to raise your standards.

Shifting lifelong patterns won't be easy, but I promise it will be worth it. The hardest part will be to make the decision to change. Once you commit to raising your standards, you will never look back. You have committed. That wet cement has dried. You've burned the ships. This is how you live now. You no longer accept your old standards of a good/fine/okay life. If doubt arises, say *no thank you*. You believe now. You are meant to feel fully alive.

Now, this is probably a pretty big shift from how you have been living, and it may come as a shock to your friends and family to see this drastic change in you. You will most likely face some resistance from your peers, friends, and family. They may try to hold you back when they see you have committed to breaking free from the norm.

Lead by example. Don't limit your life for fear of disappointing others. They can live their life their way. That does not mean you should not pursue the life you were meant to live. Treat them with compassion and continue your trajectory. Show them what you are capable of and what is possible in life. Show them what living your best life looks like. Prove

.

them wrong. Shut down the norm and refuse to let it be a part of how you live. Eventually, they will see that you no longer abide by The Okay. Who knows, you may even inspire them to see life differently and realize that more is possible than they thought. Just focus on being your best self and living your best life. The one you are now determined to live.

The insights and tool kit suggestions sprinkled throughout this book are intended to provide you with an arsenal to assist you on your adventure through life. They are the values that constitute a traveler's mindset, enabling you to let go, dream big, and live with purpose. Accept the moment before you with an open heart and you will awaken to the magic all around you. Regardless of how good or bad something may seem, choose to view it with a commitment to gratitude and trust in life's plan for you. Rise up and break free from the limitations you've set for what is possible. Your potential is unlimited.

Settling for a mediocre life is bullshit. Refuse to tolerate The Okay. Be an outlier and break free from asshole-auto-pilot. Take the leap and resolve to go all in. Trust the voice within you that is pleading for you to step up and pursue an incredible life of unbridled joy. The one you were meant to live. Raise your standards to the higher level you deserve. This epic journey through life is yours for the taking; you just have to decide to go. It's your choice. Always.

Happy travels!

ABOUT THE AUTHOR

Entrepreneur, adventurer, world traveler, and public speaker, Kat Medina has traveled to more than 35 countries, and lived in Ecuador, Argentina, France, and Spain. She draws upon her passion for travel to inspire joy in others, teaching people how to show up and live fully by embodying a traveler's mindset in daily life. She currently lives in South Lake Tahoe, California with her husband, son, and giant Golden Retriever named Donut.

ACKNOWLEDGMENTS

I pursued my long time dream of writing a book in 2019 and although I'd love to say my grit and determination was unwavering over the last several years, at times it faltered. *The Joys of Jet Lag* may not have come to shelves if it wasn't for the support and encouragement of the people in my life. This book became a literal dream come true, thanks to all of you.

Thank you to my husband, Jeff, for riding along with me during the ups and downs of the publishing rollercoaster, ceaselessly reminding me to think outside of the box and design life the way I want it. Thank you also for providing me with celebratory (and at times commiseratory) sweets and treats. I couldn't have done this without you.

Thank you to my family and a special thanks to Allie, Ryan, Mom, Debbie, Russ, Cathy, Matt, Bridget, Lisa, and Rick. And to my dad, I can't put into words how much I appreciate all that you've done. Thank you for raising me to be the woman I am. Thank you to my friends-turned-biggest cheerleaders (Leigh, Golden Girls, EOL, Lupines Ladies, The Lake Group, and all of the many other amazing people I've been lucky enough to call friends).

Thank you to Ashleigh Renard. Your guidance and coaching were invaluable and I'm so grateful for your friendship. Thank you to Carlye Adler. I recognize that time is one of our most valuable assets and you gave me so much of yours early on. It did not go unnoticed and was beyond helpful. Thank you to my incredible SLT community. Thank you to Justin and the Bare Roots crew for keeping me caffeinated (especially after all of those sleepless newborn nights). Thank you to Crazy Good Bakery for fueling my creativity in the form of pastries and pies. Thank you to Sar Dugan, Katie Arnold-Ratliff and Jamie McGillen for your help in bringing my vision to life.

Made in the USA
Monee, IL
24 October 2024

68539127R00156